# MARSE NED

### THE STORY OF AN OLD SOUTHERN FAMILY

*by*

## RITA DICKENS

*Foreword by D. B. McKay*

## EXPOSITION PRESS
### New York

Exposition Press Inc., 386 Fourth Avenue, New York 16, N.Y.

FIRST EDITION

DEDICATED

TO THE GLORY OF GOD

AND

IN LOVING MEMORY OF

MOTHER AND DADDY

# FOREWORD

MARSE NED is not only a beautiful and heart-stirring story, presented in excellent literary style, but it subtly conveys a material and truthful picture of the relations of trust—in many cases affection—existing between the gentility of the Old South and their deserving slaves. It is a truth which should be given wide dissemination in those sections of the country where hatred of the South and misrepresentation of its peoples is a reprehensible policy. I was born shortly after slavery was abolished, but I testify from personal observation to the good relations existing between the races until the advent of strife-breeders from the North.

A cherished memory of my childhood relates to my mother's devotion to her old black "mammy." At a great age the old woman was confined to her bed with an illness which proved fatal after several weeks. During her illness mother visited her every day and many nights taking her food and providing for the best medical care. At every visit she would read the Bible and sing "Aunt" Sarah's favorite hymns. And when she died her funeral was attended by many white people who knew and respected her. I have no doubt that similar instances occurred in many Southern cities and towns.

Therefore, while I have no doubt of the book's popularity in the South, I hope it will also be widely read in the North. It should be a powerful agency for the creation of good will and better understanding between the sections, with the result of closer unification as loyal Americans.

*Marse Ned* is not only calculated to stir deep emotions, but it has flashes of rich humor, and also tragedy of a nature that must excite deep sympathy.

This is Mrs. Dickens' first venture in the field of literature, but those who have the privilege of reading her book will hope that the success, which I confidently predict, will reward her and encourage her to continue writing.

D. B. McKAY

# PREFACE

FOR A LONG TIME the author has toyed with the idea of writing this book because Southern families, their way of life, and Southern Negroes and their "white folks" have a unique place in literature and in history. They have greatly enriched our country and we will be poor indeed when the last of this order have passed away. No substitute could be worthy to take their place.

Remembering one day the shortest letter her Daddy ever wrote inspired her to go on.

She was visiting relatives in Marianna, Florida, having the gay, carefree time of all teenagers. She had overstayed the time set by her parents for her departure. Every few days they would receive a letter saying: "Am leaving Monday;" next: "Staying over for a party;" again: "Be home after the dance next week," and so on and on.

Then came Daddy's exasperated letter: "Dear Daughter, For God's sake, shoot or give up the gun! Your loving Daddy."

"So," said she to herself, "I'll shoot the book or give up the gun!!"

This is not a Civil War tale, nor a genealogical chronicle, though in the beginning it necessarily touches lightly on both. Neither is it a Negro story, yet it portrays the Negroes as Southerns know and love them. It is a true story of real people, their lives and times—only the names have been changed.

Ned Blackshear of Georgia and Belle Milton of Florida portray Southern family life. Their background is important, as are some facts about the early history of Laurens County, Georgia, home of the Blackshears, and Jackson County, Florida, home of the Miltons.

For some of these early county historical facts the author is indebted to Bertha S. Hart's "Official History of Laurens County, Georgia" and to J. Randall Stanley's "History of Jackson County."

R. D.

# CHAPTER

# I

THIS IS A STORY of Southern family life — particularly the family of Ned Blackshear of Georgia and Belle Milton of Florida. It begins many years before they met, in fact before Belle was born.

General David Blackshear, grandfather of Ned, came from North Carolina and settled in Laurens County, Georgia, in 1790. He afterwards owned several thousand acres of fine river-bottom land. He owned many slaves, and was a successful planter as well as a great soldier. At thirty-nine years of age, General Blackshear married Miss Fannie Hamilton of Hancock County, Georgia. The Hamiltons were a family of great influence and position in society. David and Fannie lived at Springfield, their Laurens County plantation. When the General died in 1837 at the age of seventy-three, his vast acres were divided among his seven sons. All except one son, David, settled on their inheritance, built spacious homes and lived only a few miles from each other. David sold his acres to his brothers and migrated to Greenwood, Florida; there he married Susan Bryan, bought farm lands and slaves, and built a beautiful home and raised his family.

Edward Jefferson Blackshear, on a visit to his brother David in Greenwood, met, wooed and won Mary Jane Pittman and took her to live at Frog Level, his plantation home in Laurens County, Georgia. Mary Jane was the daughter of Colonel James J. and Martha Pittman of Marianna, Florida. Colonel Pittman was a wealthy planter from North Carolina who, in 1830, came with his wife, Martha Whitehead, to Jackson County, Florida.

He bought vast acreage and successfully operated his plantations with the help of his many slaves. Annie Eliza and John
Dawson were Mary Jane's sister and brother.

Martha Whitehead Pittman, Ned's grandmother, was an educated, cultured and pious lady of Scotch-Presbyterian faith.
She instilled religious training into her children and her slaves.
She was a good wife, a loving and ambitious mother, and a careful spender. She and her "bargains" became a family joke.

Colonel Pittman, though a staunch Presbyterian and a good
man, was less pious and more broad-minded. He was a high-
spirited, sports-loving man. His racing stable of fine horses was
famous throughout the territory, and in 1831 he organized the
first Jockey Club in Marianna where racing meets were held
twice a year. These meets were the occasion for many social
events to entertain the elite who came from neighboring towns
to enter their horses in the races, to try their luck at the gaming
tables and to enjoy the parties and dances. Captain Hezekiah
Wilder from Quincy was Colonel Pittman's friendly racing
rival. These two thought nothing of betting five hundred dollars on a single race between their horses. Gaiety reigned supreme!

It was during the festivities of one of Colonel Pittman's
racing meets that Edward Jefferson Blackshear met Mary Jane
Pittman whom he later married.

The Blackshears were cultured, educated people—they
possessed "uncommon vigor of mind and great practical sense."
The Blackshear lands in Laurens County were among the finest
farming sections of the South, situated in the heart of Georgia's
agricultural district, on the east side of the Oconee River. Dublin, the county seat, is on the west bank. No landmark is more
fascinating and more romantic than the old flat-bottom river
ferry known as Blackshear's Ferry, located four and a half miles
north of Dublin. It has carried its mechanical, human and animal
cargoes for more than a century. Many generations and many
races—red man, white man, black man—have depended upon it.
The first mention of a ferry was made in county records dated
February 2, 1808: "Ordered that a ferry be established across the

Oconee River at Blackshear's landing at the following rates: for
a loaded wagon 50 cents, an empty wagon 37½ cents, loaded
cart 25 cents, empty cart 18¾ cents, pleasure carriage with
waiter and horses 37½ cents, man and horse 6¼ cents, led
horse and footman, all black cattle 2 cents per head, sheep, hogs
and goats 1 cent each."

# CHAPTER

# II

In 1845 JOHN MILTON, Florida's future Civil War governor, son of General Homer Virgil Milton of Louisville, Georgia, and his wife Susan Amanda Cobb, came to Jackson County, Florida, and settled near Marianna on his plantation "Sylvania," consisting of 7,326 acres. His fifty-two slaves tilled the soil and supplied the house servants.

One of their sons, Major William Henry Milton, and his wife, Lucy Hearn, were the parents of Belle Milton. Their lovely spacious home was in Marianna.

Situated on the west bank of the beautiful Chipola River, Marianna was a rich man's town. Many men of wealth and high educational attainments settled there in the 1830's with their cultured wives. They came mainly from Georgia and Alabama, but many merchants and professional men came from Northern states. These early Jackson County pioneers represented a class of citizens seldom, if ever, found on an American frontier. The soil was rich and fertile and produced premium crops. Its verdant pine forests furnished naval stores in commercial quantity. The limestone rock foundation was ideal for quarries from which limestone blocks were dug and used in the erection of many buildings. One of Florida's natural wonders is beautiful and romantic Blue Springs. A tremendous volume of cold water flows through two orifices, so clear that fish can be seen swimming playfully far below the surface. It creates a pond several miles in length and turned the wheels of historic Merritt's grist mill. Blue Springs and Merritt's Mill Pond have always been favorite picnic grounds. The road to Blue Springs was a natural "lovers' lane" with its huge overlapping water oaks festooned with garlands of long gray moss. Young men for generations have wooed their sweethearts on that road.

Society in Laurens and Jackson Counties in ante-bellum days was shaped by the wealth and culture of the plantation families. They built large and pretentious homes adorned with columns and iron grille work. The rooms were large, the halls built wide for dances, the verandas spacious with steps often running the full length of the veranda. Hospitality was dispensed on a lavish and magnificent scale entirely unknown to future generations.

At the rear of these homes were other houses—the overseer's dwelling and office, barns, blacksmith shop, the inevitable cotton gin, the smokehouse where meat was cured and kept, big clay banks where sweet potatoes were stored and kept through the winter, the cane mill, which was horse-propelled, and the huge kettles or vats for boiling the cane juice into syrup. These vats were set in and over a brick fireplace with a chimney at the back and the fire was built under the vat. About a half-mile further back were the slave quarters, a row or semi-circle of two- and three-room cabins that housed the Negroes. There were vast orchards of fruit trees and extensive vineyards of grapes for wine-making. The remaining vast acreage was planted in cotton, the most important money crop; and in corn, peanuts, potatoes, sugar cane and all vegetables and commodities necessary for plantation living.

The slaves were the Negro aristocracy of the ante-bellum period. Their status in the master's home closely resembled that of a member of the family. They were well treated and greatly beloved. They' served gladly, faithfully and loyally. Much has been written of the devotion of the slaves to the children of their masters. "Mammy" tended them from infancy, but she intuitively knew when to start addressing her charges as "Mister" or "Miss."

The slaves looked upon the free Negro with contempt and pitied him as a "poor fellow who has no master." A free Negro was not welcome and had no place in the social or economic system. Many of them chose their own master and voluntarily went into slavery. Without slaves, the romantic "Golden Age" of the ante-bellum era would not have flourished. This aristocracy disappeared when its foundation of slavery was outlawed.

EDWARD BLACKSHEAR and Mary Jane Pittman had four children, all born at Frog Level. Mary, the oldest, and Edward Jefferson, Jr., the youngest, survived, though the birth of "little Ned" cost his mother's life. He was six weeks old when she died.

Grandma Pittman made the long and hazardous trip from Florida to Georgia to see about Mary Jane's children. There were no railroads in Jackson County prior to 1881. She went by stagecoach or private conveyance to Neal's Landing—an important shipping point for cargo, freight and passengers. This landing is situated in the northeast section of Jackson County on the Chattahoochee and Apalachicola rivers. Picturesque steamboats plied up and down these rivers. At Neal's Landing, Grandma Pittman took a steamboat to Columbus, Georgia, thence on crude and uncomfortable trains to the little "whistle stop" at Oconee, Georgia. There she was met by the Blackshear coachman and driven to Frog Level. Connections were bad and it took many days to complete the trip, therefore her visits were of several months' duration.

There were many problems to be solved and adjustments to be made after Mary Jane's death. It was agreed that Mary should return to Florida with Grandma, but Ned's father would not part with his baby son. Care and feeding arrangements had to be made for him. There were no canned milk and baby foods in those days, so this problem was solved by bringing Marthy, a slave who had a few days previously given still-birth to her baby, into the house to wet-nurse young Ned. To use her words, she "suckled Marse Ned"—all the slaves affectionately called him Marse Ned.

Marthy was fed a special diet in the kitchen, one suitable to agree with and not "colic" the baby, and this diet she did not relish. One day Marthy stealthily took Ned to her cabin where she had concealed a watermelon. She laid him on her bed, and as she eagerly cut the melon she said—stuttering more than usual in her excitement—"M-m-m-arse N-n-ed, effen dis w-w-watermelon is gwine to k-k-kill yo', yo' is gw-gw-gwine to die, kaze I sho' is gw-gw-gwine eat dis m-m-melon!" Needless to say, Ned lived.

Hannah was brought up from the slave quarters and established as housekeeper and general manager of all household servants. Reuben, the most beloved of all the slaves, was the cotton ginner and self-appointed counselor of the darkies. They all loved and respected him and his master trusted him implicitly.

Ned's father was a busy planter, State Senator and County Judge, and he had little time for and less knowledge of the care of a baby. When Grandma and Mary left for Florida, Ned was entrusted to Hannah, Reuben and Marthy, all of whom adored him. Except for their loving care, he, like Topsy, "just growed" into a beautiful robust little boy, with big trusting blue eyes, blond hair and a heavenly smile. He had the run of the plantation yard and out-buildings. Wherever he went the Negroes were careful to see that no harm befell Marse Ned. In their sight he could do no wrong. He absorbed their superstitions, simple faith, homely philosophy and imagination. Through them he developed a deep love not only for the Negro but for all humanity. These deep-rooted traits stayed with him throughout his long life and were instrumental in developing him into the lovable, unique and unforgettable character that he became.

All of the Negroes were afraid of the supernatural, especially of cemeteries—"grave-yards" they called them. One day Uncle Reuben was sent on an errand to Blackshear's grist mill. There he was delayed until after dark. On the way home he had to pass the cemetery. He arrived home on the run and out of breath. The Negroes chorused, "Uncle Reuben, what you runnin' frum?"

He, panting, replied, "Reuben started to run when he passed dat grave-yard, but he was sho 'nuff runnin' when he seen dat field o' bear-grass lookin' white lak a ghost an' de wind a-wavin' it at me in de moonlight."

The darkies laughed and said, "You ain' skeered o' bear-grass, is yo'?"

"Well," he answered, "Reuben was done skeered 'fo' he got to dat field, an' when Reuben is done skeered he's jes' as skeered o' bear-grass as he is o' anythin' else!"

GRANDMA PITTMAN and young Mary came every year to Frog
Level. Those were wonderful months for Ned though Grandma
put him through rigid training in "manners," but she rewarded
him by reading aloud all the good books available. When Grandma was there she was mistress of the plantation. The slaves
adored "Ole Miss." Like all noble Southern women, she had
compassion for the slaves and ministered to them in sickness,
sorrow and old age. Her solicitude and interest and pious instruction inspired their devotion and loyalty. These qualities in
the Southern mistresses were largely responsible for many slaves
remaining faithful and loyal during and after the trying days
of the 1860's.

In the evenings Grandma, Pa, Mary and Ned would sit on
the veranda and enjoy the sweet-sad spirituals wafted by the
breeze from the Negro cabins. These Negro songs were the first
things Ned learned to play, by ear, on his father's old violin.
He had a sweet voice and often joined in the Negro songs.

Appreciating his talent, Grandma decided when Ned was ten
years old that he should have music lessons. A German peddler-
musician arrived at Frog Level one late stormy afternoon and
was invited to spend the night. Thrifty Grandma, always hunting a "bargain," traded with the "professor" to stay and give
Ned violin lessons in exchange for six months' room and board.

Next morning Ned went into the parlor for his first lesson.
The "professor", standing there in his long black coat, oft-
mended trousers and spats over his rather derelict shoes, was
anxious to teach this boy—motivated not so much by love of

music or children, but by the fact that Frog Level would be a comfortable home during the coming winter.

Patronizingly he asked young Ned, "Do you know what a note is, boy?"

Ned's candid eyes looked up at the "professor" and he proudly answered, "Yessir, Pa sent a note by me yesterday to Uncle Everard."

"Humph," the "professor" grunted. "Do you know what a key is?"

"Yessir, I know the old smokehouse key!" Ned was pleased that the questions were so easy.

The "professor," determined to keep his new-found home, tried once more. "Do you know what a chord is?"

Ned did not hesitate. "Yessir. I helped stack all those cords of wood in the back yard!"

There the "music" lesson ended—the "professor," dazed and in utter defeat, and Ned pleased to have known all the answers. The next morning the "professor" packed his wares and sorrowfully moved on, a peddler once more.

This was not the end of the violin for Ned. His soul was so full of music it had to find expression. With a true musical ear and a perfect memory he learned to play correctly any composition that he heard. He had a gift for the violin comparable to that which the famous Negro "Blind Tom" had for the piano.

CHAPTER

V

GRANDMA GAVE FREQUENT week-end houseparties at Frog Level for Mary, who was growing into a beautiful young lady. Friends and relatives came from all the plantations for miles around to join in the gaiety. Travel was long and arduous in those days, and such parties necessarily lasted two or three days, as few lived close enough to make the round trip in a single day. Entire families came, with their personal servants and coachmen. The host's coachman played host in the Negro quarter to the visiting servants, and each tried to outdo the other in "manners" and politeness, to reflect all credit possible on their beloved "white folks" and the training they had received from them.

Though Ned was a bit young to enjoy dancing with the girls and sitting with them on the veranda in the moonlight, he loved the music and the festive mood, not to mention the endless supply of food.

Though children of that era were usually "seen but not heard," Ned was a born teller-of-tales. One evening at dinner, he had the guests convulsed with laughter at one of his experiences earlier that day. He had been sent to the quarter with a message for one of the coachmen as to his master's departure and arrived as the servants were having their dinner.

Uncle Reuben, at the head of the table, was speaking to one of the guests, "Have a 'tater, Zeke?"

"Not jes' now, thank yo', Uncle Reuben," the guest replied.

In his most gracious manner, Uncle Reuben said, "Look

here, Nigger, effen yo' wants a tater, take it now. Don' come 'ere both'in' me when I gits to eatin'."

Ned's cousin Tom, near his own age, was always one of the guests at these parties, and they spent many boyhood hours "exploring" every nook and cranny of the plantation.

One day Ned and Tom were playing around inside the cotton gin, getting in Uncle Reuben's way and worrying him because he knew the danger for them there, but he could not persuade them to leave. Finally Uncle Reuben walked out and started down the path. The boys ran after him, and Ned said, "Where are you going, Uncle Reuben?"

"I'se gwine to my cabin, kaze I ain't got no mo' business here since Marster done hired hisself two new ginners."

He kept on walking and so did the boys, begging Uncle Reuben to go back. After much persuasion and many boyish promises, Uncle Reuben returned to his work in the gin, and he had no more trouble with "Marster's two new ginners."

Ned idolized Uncle Reuben. As he sat on the cabin steps one late afternoon listening to Uncle Reuben spin tales for his amusement, Ned said, "When I get grown I want to be just like you, Uncle Reuben."

"Bless de Lawd, chile," Uncle Reuben exploded, "don' neber say dat agin! You is got to be a gen'l'man like yo' pa. You is a born gen'l'man—not no po' white trash—and don' you nevah fo'git it. Ol' Reuben's proud o' his white folks and his Marse Ned, and I ain' gwine have you tryin' to be lak no nigger."

"Uncle Reuben," asked Ned, "why am I white and you black, anyway? Grandma said God made everybody. Why did he make folks different?"

"Chile, de good Lawd knowed what he was a-doin', an' it ain't up to nobody to try to make it diffunt." Uncle Reuben frowned in concentration, trying to answer the boy's questions with his limited knowledge so that the boy would understand.

"Marse Ned, you see dem chickens an' ducks an' turkeys an' geese out dere in de chicken yard? God made dem, too. Dey runs aroun' dat pen all in a bunch, but dey don' mix themselves up. De gobblers mates wid de turkey hens, an' de roosters wid de chickens; dem ducks an' geese do de same thing. You know what would happen effen dey didn't? A egg would hatch out sump'n' wid a head lak a turkey an' a tail lak a duck, an' it'd be a freak—wouldn't none o' the mothers have nuthin' to do wid it. Well, de Lawd means folks to do de same thing. He loves His white chillun an' His black chillun, but He made 'em diffunt an 'cordin' to God's plan dey's s'posed to stay diffunt."

Young Ned listened raptly as the old darky talked on.

"An' it ain't jes' de yard animals, Marse Ned. De wild uns is de same. De fish in de sea an' de birds in de air does de same. Eben de snakes in de bottom land crawls aroun' in de same sun an' sheds dey skin de same way—but dey don' mix up at matin' time, nawsuh. An' dat's de way de Lawd 'tends it to be wid folks, too, an' don' you fo'git it, boy."

"I won't, Uncle Reuben," Ned answered.

"Now you git along up to de big house, boy. Ole Miss she gwine be wantin' you to git yo' supper, an' I got work to do."

Ned didn't go at his usual trot but walked toward the house in a pensive mood, reflecting on the old darky's words, with questions still unanswered. But at supper there was no chance to pursue the matter with Pa or Grandma. In the mail that day was a letter from Grandma's youngest son John, just 17, who was attending the University of Virginia, and nothing would do but that she read the letter aloud.

*University of Virginia*
*October 4, 1860*

MY DEAR MOTHER,

I wrote you a letter some time ago but have not received an answer. As you desire me to write often, I will not stand upon ceremony, especially when you wish to hear from me.

When I wrote you my last I had not entered the University but I am now a regular student. I have taken the schools of Latin, Mathematics and Moral Philosophy. I will graduate in all three in the course of three years. It requires longer to graduate in Mathematics than in any other school in the University. They call each study a school here. It is more difficult to graduate here than any other institution in the United States. The reason of it is that nearly all the other institutions require you to go a certain number of years on a prescribed course; if you elect your studies in them you are counted irregular. But here you can select any studies you please. You do not graduate on them as a whole like at other colleges, but on each one separately. This is the reason why it is more difficult to graduate here than elsewhere.

I wrote you that after I bought my clothes I had barely enough money to enter the University. I need about fifty or a hundred dollars. Please send it on to me immediately. Take the money to Tarboro and buy a check on New York. I cannot get along comfortably without it. If you send me that I will not need any more in a long time. Please send the money for I have not a cent. Write soon to your affectionate son,

JOHN D. PITTMAN

Pa laughed, "Just like a boy, always needing money. I'll see to getting the check for you tomorrow, Mrs. Pittman."

"Thank you, Mr. Blackshear. Now if you will excuse me I'll leave you to your cigar and brandy. Come, Ned, it's off to bed for you, young man."

Ned rose obediently but reluctantly, wishing he was a grown man and could enjoy cigars and brandy after supper with his father.

Finally in bed, Ned's thoughts returned to his talk that afternoon with Uncle Reuben. Grandma came in to say good night, and asked if he had said his prayers.

"Yes'm," he replied, and before she could leave the room he hurriedly asked, "Grandma, why did God make some people white and some black?"

Somewhat startled by the suddenness of his question, Grandma asked Ned, "What brought this up?"

He told her of his talk with Uncle Reuben. Grandma pulled the little rocking chair close to Ned's bed and sat down. "It's all in the Bible, Ned. Do you remember the story of Noah and the Ark?"

"I sure do. It rained and rained, and Noah took his family and two of every kind of animal on the Ark so they'd be saved."

"Yes. Well, after the flood was over they all came out of the Ark and started life again on land, and the earth was re-peopled by Noah's descendants. Well, one of Noah's sons, Ham—he was named that because in their language the word 'Ham' meant swarthy, or dark-colored—did a shameful deed and when Noah found out about it he was very angry. He cursed Ham and put a curse on Ham's son, Canaan, saying 'A servant of servants shall he be unto his brethren.' And when the land of their habitation was divided among Noah and his sons, Ham and Canaan were given that part of the land that is now Egypt, in Africa. They were the ancestors of the Negroes who were brought in boats from Africa to America by Yankee traders and sold to the Southern planters to help farm the big plantations."

"I'm glad we got Uncle Reuben, Grandma, aren't you," smiled the boy.

"Yes, son, I am. Uncle Reuben is a good man and a faithful servant as well as a loyal friend. Ned, always remember that the Negroes are a proud and noble people, and treat them fairly and justly. Respect their rights as human beings, and reward them for their good deeds. Yet never forget that God made Negroes and white people different. We don't look alike, think, talk, sing or act alike."

Ned laughed. "And we sure don't smell alike, Grandma."

Grandma smiled, then put the conversation to an end as she blew out the lamp and kissed Ned good night.

CHAPTER

# VI

SUNDAY MORNING came bright and crisp this fall day and the plantation was stirring early with preparations for the big day. While the family was at breakfast they heard a commotion in the back yard. Mr. Blackshear strode to the back porch, along with Grandma, Mary and Ned, to see what was up. Some of the slaves were grouped about the old clay "tater bank" arguing over who would go in to get the "taters." It was a rule that the old crop must be used before they could start on the new one, and this time of year the almost empty clay bank showed signs of caving in. None of the slaves wanted to risk going in for the potatoes.

Uncle Reuben, exasperated with the younger darkies, said "Reuben's gwine have his taters!"

He got down on his hands and knees and started backwards into the bank. One of the Negro boys called out, "Why you backin' in dat bank?"

They all laughed, but Uncle Reuben looked at them quite seriously and said, "Effen dis bank's gwine cave in, Reuben wants dat end out what can tell about it!"

Pa and the family joined in the laughter, then, seeing that the situation was under control, started into the house.

Tempie, one of the younger Negro girls—the one the other slaves called "Blue-Gum Tempie"—ran over to the edge of the porch. Taking advantage of Pa's good humor, she asked, "Marster, kin I have a ration o' meat today?"

Pa, knowing full well that rations were issued to the slaves on Saturday, said, "Weren't you given a two-day ration of meat yesterday?"

Tempie grinned, her eyes wide, as she said, "Yassuh, Marster, but I swear fo' Gawd dat meat done swunk!"

Ned was sure the people on the next plantation heard Pa's resounding laugh as he told Grandma to have Hannah give Tempie the meat ration.

Soon it was time for church. The Blackshears attended Boiling Springs Methodist Church one Sunday a month—a preacher served many country churches in those days, and travel being by foot, carriage or horseback in the rural areas, one Sunday a month was all he could manage for each church. The country church was not only the religious center of the community but doubled as a social center. Here the neighboring families met to worship, break bread, and exchange news of family and friends, war and politics, planting and economics. The plantation kitchens were beehives of activity for days before "Church Sunday" with the preparation of the bounteous baskets of food that would be spread on the wooden tables under the trees.

After the service the Negroes who had driven the families to church—they sat in the servants' gallery taking part in the service and listening to the sermon—brought forth the well-laden picnic baskets from the carriages and wagons, laid snowy linen cloths on the crude tables built under the trees, and spread the finest dinner imaginable. Such laughing and talking and feasting as went on!

While dinner was being spread, the children romped and played and swung from the trees and "joggled" on the joggling board. The young girls and their beaus would pair off and walk down to the spring, whispering "sweet nothings" to each other. Ned noticed that Mary and Cince Guyton always walked together.

The men gathered as usual under their favorite tree, today's main topic being the recent suicide of an acquaintance in the next county. Each man had his own views on what happens to a man's soul when he takes his own life. Pa's overseer, a respected, though illiterate, man, joined the group and Pa turned to him, saying, "Brown, what do you think of a man who commits suicide?"

Brown replied, in all seriousness, "Well, Sir, I think he ought to be made to support the child!"

Ned and his group of boy friends were about a year too young and a bit too shy to walk to the spring with girls, but they did a lot of talking about girls they liked. They sat on the ground playing mumble-peg and exchanging confidences about the kind of a girl they would marry. One wanted a beautiful blonde, another chose a fiery redhead, the next wanted a brunette and she must be a good cook, and so on and on they voiced their choices. One of the boys, Coot Spence, was a bit older than the rest, homely, and more than a little simple-minded. Coot had said nothing until Ned prodded him.

"Come on, Coot, tell us what kind of girl you are going to marry."

"Well, boys," he answered in his nasal voice, "just give me the gal that loves Coot Spence."

Years later when Ned told this story he said, "I'll be dog-goned if old Coot didn't show more sense than all of us!"

After returning home from church Grandma walked to the Negro quarter to take some boiled custard to Aunt Dicey, a sick and aging slave. Theeny and Dinah were sitting on the cabin steps, and when Grandma returned to the house she was chuckling over their conversation that they hadn't realized she could hear. Grandma sat down and, laughing, told Pa he might find a new slave in the quarter before long.

"Why?" asked Pa.

"Theeny asked Dinah 'Who was that strange Nigger passed by the field yestiddy when we wuz choppin' cotton near de fence?' Dinah said 'I don' know but he'll be back.' When Theeny asked how she was so sure, Dinah rolled her head back, looked up at the sky and confidently said, 'Kaze I done seed de white o' his eye!' "

# VII

ONE NIGHT old Aunt Dicey passed away. Grandma had seen that she had had good care and ministered personally to some of her needs. The cotton ginning season being over, Uncle Reuben was elected to dig Aunt Dicey's grave.

Uncle Reuben was "plumb skeered" to go to "dat grave-yard" alone. He begged, pleaded and cajoled with the other darkies for "'jes' one o' you come go wid me, jes' to keep me company—Reuben will do the diggin'.'"

They were all as scared of a cemetery as Reuben was, so none of them would go. Finally, Reuben picked up a pickaninny from the ground, swung him to his shoulder and started on his way. The others, aghast, called out, "Lawd, Gawd, Reuben, what you gwine do wid dat baby?"

"Well, he's 'somebody'!" And he kept right on walking toward his gruesome job.

Next day came another letter from John from the University and the family listened eagerly as Grandma read it aloud:

*University of Virginia*
*October 17, 1860*

MY DEAR MOTHER,

The longer I remain at the University the better I like it. The accommodations of students are not as great as they should be, but so far as the instruction is concerned everything is complete. I delight in the study of Moral Philosophy. The Professor of the school is the celebrated Presbyterian minister, Dr. W. H. McGuffey. I attend his Bible class every Sunday. He is now lecturing on the Psalms.

A day or two ago Blue Ridge Mountain was covered with snow. My room is a quarter of a mile from the lecture rooms. I will have a time walking on snow this winter. I came so unprepared for the winters they have here. I will spend more money this session than I expected. I bought a substantial winter's outfit in Richmond, Va. I assure you I am just as economical as comfort will allow. By the time I get home next summer I will have spent a little over five hundred dollars. Next session I will spend $150.00 less than I will this session. I will buy all my clothes, boots and shoes before I leave home then will be obliged to buy only a few things here. I make these statements because I do not wish you to think that my expenses every year will be as much as they will be this session. I will have $88.00 more to pay on my board. We make the payments for board, $44.00 when you first come, $44.00 the first of January and $44.00 the first of April. Be sure to send this money next December.

The dinner bell has rung. Give my love to all. Your affectionate son,

JOHN D. PITTMAN

As she folded the letter there was a wistful look about her, but only for a moment. With a sigh, she asked Pa, "Do you suppose, Mr. Blackshear, he didn't receive the money I sent?"

"The mails are slow, Mrs. Pittman," Pa reminded her, "perhaps he received it after posting that letter."

"I suppose you are right. It has taken a long time for this letter to get here, but I note he addressed me at Cousin Higgs's in North Carolina and they sent it on to me," mused Grandma.

In a few days, Pa's guess proved right. Another letter came from John.

*University of Virginia*
*November 6, 1860*

MY DEAR MA,

I wrote you a letter to North Carolina. Received your letter from Georgia and was surprised to learn you had left North Carolina.

I am sorry Willie Higgs would not go home with you. I felt certain that one of the boys would go. I am very uneasy about you going to Florida by yourself, am afraid something will happen on the way. I would not have been willing to leave you in North Carolina if I'd known you would be obliged to go home by yourself.

I am sorry to hear you could not pass your North Carolina money in Georgia. I received the check you sent me but failed to mention it in my last letter.

Today is election day and I reckon Lincoln will be elected. If he is I reckon we will have to quit this University, take muskets and go to fighting. I hope this will not be. We will know tomorrow whether Lincoln is elected. If he carries the State of New York he will be the next President.

I am as ever your affectionate son,

JOHN D. PITTMAN

John's reference to the election brought a hush around the room. Every Southern plantation owner felt strong apprehension over their beloved lands and homes, families and slaves if Mr. Lincoln was elected and his party in power. Pa was sorely troubled and walked out in the yard to think. Seeing Uncle Reuben closing the barn door, Pa called to him. Uncle Reuben, pulling his battered old hat off his kinky grey head, came over.

"Uncle Reuben, there's trouble ahead for all of us, I'm afraid," Pa said.

"Yassuh, Marster, I'se heerd talk, but I don't reckon I understan's jes' what it all means."

"If Mr. Lincoln is elected president, Uncle Reuben, they may try to make us set our slaves free. If they do, there'll be a war, young men will be killed—fighting for the way of life they know and love and believe in," Pa explained.

Uncle Reuben heard only the words "set our slaves free." He looked frightened yet indignant as he said, "Marster, is dey gwine take us 'way frum our white folks? Oh, Lawd Gawd, what's gwine happen to us iffen dey does dat? Who gwine tend us when we git old an' sick an' hongry, Marster, 'cept our white folks dat loves us?"

"Now, Uncle Reuben," said Pa, "don't get upset. It hasn't happened yet, though I fear that it might. In the meantime, try not to worry."

"Us niggers don' know how to worry, Marster—it's jes' 'go

day, come day, God sen' Sunday' wid us, 'cause Gawd an' de white folks has allus took keer o' us."

"Well, we'll all hope and pray, Uncle Reuben, and do the best we can," said Pa reassuringly.

Time passed quickly at Frog Level and Grandma and Mary were getting things in order before returning to Marianna. It had been a long, cold winter and spring was a little late arriving. Travel conditions being as they were, it was nearly mid-April before their departure. The day before they were to leave, another letter came from John which Grandma read aloud to the family, as usual.

> Lynchburg, Va.
> April 1, 1861

My dear Mother,

I received your letter a few days ago in which you expressed great uneasiness about my health. My health is improving. I have quit confining myself so closely and take more exercise. I do not study so hard as formerly. About leaving the University and going to Marietta, we will talk that over next summer, but I am not willing to go there. I like this school very much. There is very little intemperance. A boy is not governed much after he leaves the lecture room, he is left to his own honor. If he does anything very mean they will expel him.

At the exams in the different schools they put up some questions on the blackboard and you return written answers to the professors. They value the questions at so much and your answers according to the same system. If the values of your answers to the questions equal three-fourths of the values of the questions they will give you a diploma. If not, they will "pitch" you, as the students say. They will not graduate a boy unless he understands the subject. There were 170 students in the Moral Philosophy class last year and only 34 graduated. Mr. Dudley teaches Latin, Mr. Bledso (or Strother) teaches Mathematics and Dr. Wm. H. McGuffey Moral Philosophy. I like them all very well but I like Dr. McGuffey the best. I attend the Methodist Church more than any other. The Chaplain of the University is a Methodist. The Chaplain will be a Baptist next session. I sometimes go down town to the Presbyterian Church. Charlottesville is about a mile from the University.

The boys whom I'm best acquainted with are two Erwings from Tennessee, Dixon from Mississippi, Wimberly and Garrison from Georgia. Wimberly is from near Irwington, Georgia.

My fare is poor. I board at the worst eating house in college. I don't get anything good and what I do get is not clean. I cannot change my eating house because I board in college and so many rooms are given to each hotel keeper. Next session they will let the boys eat where they please then the fare will be better. I intend to board with Dr. McKenzie next session. His is a private boarding house.

The last day of the session is July 4th. I will leave for home the 5th. You better send me a check for $150.00 that will pay my little debts and leave me some money after I get home. That will make $650.00 I've had since I left you in North Carolina. Very few get through here for less than $600.00 the first year.

Love to all, write soon. Your affectionate son,

JOHN D. PITTMAN

# VIII

NED MISSED GRANDMA and Mary very much, but managed to find plenty of things to do to occupy his time. Yet he and Pa looked forward to the time when the "women folks" would be with them again. In late summer, the family was saddened by news of Grandpa Pittman's death after a brief illness. Grandma wrote that John got home from school in time, and that Grandpa had known him and had even been able to show interest in the boy's life at school. She and Mary would not come to Frog Level until after Thanksgiving as John would be at home until October and there were many extra duties for her to see about at the plantation.

When they finally arrived, Ned went with the coachman to Oconee to meet them, and it was a happy reunion. He and Grandma adored each other!

"Did you see any alligators on the boat trip, Grandma?" asked Ned on the way home.

"Yes, we did." Grandma laughed. "There was a Yankee and his wife on the boat and they had never seen an alligator before. The man asked the Captain if the alligator was an amphibious animal, and the Captain unhesitatingly replied 'Yes, sir! He'll eat a hog in a minute!' "

Amid such laughter, the carriage arrived at Frog Level, and the family and servants all assumed a feeling of joy and contentment now that Ole Miss and Miss Mary were with them once more.

Shortly after their arrival came John's letter telling of his trip back to school. Grandma read it to the family after dinner:

*Lynchburg, Va.*
*October, 1861*

MY DEAR MOTHER,

I have gotten this far on my journey. I was bothered somewhat in getting here. I missed a great many connections. I lost a little money on account of unavoidable circumstances. It seems the fates are opposed to my going to the University of Virginia. I will tell you something about my journey.

I reached Hodgson's Landing about 12 o'clock on Saturday. There I was informed that the steamer Jackson was a day behind time and would not pass until Sunday evening. I had to pay Mr. Hodgson $2.00 to keep me over. Bad luck No. 1. I had a fine time with Fannie B. and Molly B. I found the latter all that Aunt Peggy had represented. She will graduate next summer. She will be "going, going, gone" before I quit school. I arrived at Fort Gaines about 5 o'clock Monday A.M. We met the steamer Wayne at Ft. Gaines. She was going to the Bay. She had some cannon for the soldiers on the island. They speak of moving the soldiers from that place. I was compelled to pay a man $1.00 for taking my baggage from the landing to the depot, he would not do it for less, so that was bad luck No. 2. I went to the hotel where I fortunately met Mr. Grist. He invited me to go to his home but I did not have time. I sent my respects to the boys and to Mrs. Wadlaw. Mrs. Wakefield and Miss Augusta are in Macon.

After leaving Ft. Gaines I went direct to Macon. There is no night train from Macon to Atlanta so I was compelled to stay at Macon all night. I rested at Brown's Hotel near the depot. I paid $1.25 for that rest—bad luck No. 3. The cars left Macon very early Tuesday A.M. and I reached Atlanta about 4 P.M. that same day. I left Atlanta Tuesday evening 7 o'clock and arrived at Knoxville, Tenn., Wednesday morning. I felt like I was in the enemy's country while I was passing through East Tenn. That is old John Brown's region. I left Knoxville Wednesday A.M. and reached Bristol in the evening. While going I began to nod and the first thing I knew my hat flew out the window. I will never see that hat again. I never succeeded in getting a hat until I reached Lynchburg. I gave $2.50 for a new hat. Bad luck No. 4. I left Bristol Tuesday evening and arrived at Lynchburg, Va., at 10 o'clock Thursday A.M. The train was due at 6 A.M. so I missed the connection and am obliged to lay over here until tomorrow (Friday) morning. I will get to Charlottesville sometime tomorrow. Not getting to Lynchburg in time is bad luck No. 5 for I will be compelled to pay a tavern bill.

There are plenty of good corn crops in East Tennessee. I came over the Blue Ridge Mountains by a gradual ascent. We passed through three tunnels; they were as dark as Egypt.

There is *no* school at Emory and at Henry College, Va. I am afraid we will have a thin school at the University of Virginia. We have no right to expect more than 200 students.

Give my love to all. Write soon. Direct to the University of Virginia. Your affectionate son,

JOHN D. PITTMAN

Grandma was worried about John, though she tried hard not to show it. Nevertheless, she was obviously relieved to hear again from John that he had reached school safely. She read the letter to Pa, Mary and Ned.

*University of Virginia*
*Oct. 17th, 1861*

MY DEAR MOTHER,

I reached the University in safety. I went down to the U. the same day and found only 20 or 30 students. I expected to find about 100. Imagine then how completely by surprise I was taken. War has certainly made its impress upon this once favored institution. The students still come in. We have now about 50 students. The professors think there will be about 150 by the middle of the session. The Board of Visitors that met in order to appoint a military professor could not succeed in making a suitable appointment. Consequently we have no military school as yet; but Prof. M. Schele DeVane, who was an officer in the Russian War, is trying to get up a military school on his own "hook." I reckon he will succeed; if he does not, the students intend to get up a company, so I will have the chance of studying tactics in one way or another. If they do not succeed in getting the military school, I will be sorry I did not go to Marietta, for I have a great desire to learn tactics.

There are a great many sick soldiers here. All the wounded soldiers have been taken from the University and there is no sign of their having been there. Some of the wounded Yankees who were carried to Richmond were allowed to go home. While they were at Richmond they pretended to have a great affection for the South, but as soon as they got North they commenced abusing the South, and declared that the Southerners had treated them like dogs. These are the thanks we received for our great kindness.

A great many soldiers are hopping about the University, some have their legs and others their arms cut off. It must be some consolation to them to know they lost their limbs in the defense of their country. Everybody is for the South up here; you don't hear any grumbling as you do in Marianna. Everybody works for the support of the soldiers, the ladies, especially, who do as much for the South as the men. Honor to the ladies!

I board at Mrs. McKenzie's, a widow, and a nice lady she is too. Her son who is married and keeps the University book stores lives with her. I pay $20.00 per month for board. For this Mrs. McKenzie provides me with a room and a servant to clean it up, bring me water, make up my fire and black my shoes. She also furnished my room. I pay for lights and fuel. I can board at other houses for $10 or $12 cheaper, but I would not leave Mrs. McKenzie's. She gives us a plenty of everything good to eat, and she treats her boarders as if they were her sons. She nurses them when they get sick. My board will be $180.00 for nine moths. Write soon, give my love to all. Your affectionate son,

JOHN D. PITTMAN

When she finished reading, Pa said, "Mrs. Pittman, I fear the boy will not be able to finish his schooling. This dreadful war is certainly taking its toll of the South's young men."

"Yes, Mr. Blackshear, I know," she said. "John will do his best at the University, I know. Yet, like all young men at this time, he is eager to fight for his country and his ideals. I can only hope and pray and leave the outcome to God."

Though the holiday season was at hand, war had touched each family on all the neighboring plantations. News of battles traveled slowly, however, and each family made every effort to make the holiday a festive one, hoping the husbands and sons would get leave to come home. Ned's sister Mary made frequent visits to the Guyton plantation, hoping for news of Cince.

By now most of the South's young men—many accompanied by a faithful slave who often performed heroic services—were in the Confederate Army. Others were talking of joining the forces and the boys were fretting over being too young to go to war. The mothers and young wives and sweethearts were filled with apprehension, but they sent their men off with a smile and "carried on" as best they could without them. Many prayers were said in churches and in homes for the "safety of our boys who are fighting the Yankees for what we and they believe to be a just cause."

Young Ned was now beginning to comprehend some of the war talk, and the war news in John's letters was very interesting to him. When the next letter came, Ned ran to take it to Grandma and insisted that she read it right that minute—which, of course, she was also anxious to do. She sat down, took her spectacles from her apron pocket, and began to read:

*University of Virginia*
*Nov. 18th, 1861*

MY DEAR MOTHER:

I was delighted to receive your letter a few days ago. I am very glad you sent the $2.00 in gold, for it is very hard to get any money for postage. I have a great many things to write about but I don't know which to begin with.

There are a great many sick soldiers here. 200 were brought up a few days ago. The Southern Confederate Hospital is just opposite Mrs. McKenzie's. All the professors at the University attend the hospital. They are very kind and the sick soldiers are thankful for any little act of kindness. A great many of those who were not so badly wounded at Manassas go home to see their friends. Last Saturday everybody believed there would be another fight at Manassas. The dispatch said that all our pickets had been driven in, and our Generals had ordered their men to sleep on their arms and be ready for battle at a moment's warning. All were excited in Charlottesville, and a great many of the citizens prepared to go down and take part in the engagement. But the battle did not take place, and everybody was disappointed rather than otherwise. Last night a dispatch came which said that Mason and Slidell, our commissioners to Europe, have been taken prisoners while sailing under a British flag. It is said that they have been carried to Fortress Monroe. I hope this is a false report. If true, the editors are to blame. They published all about the sailing of our commissioners—where they landed, where they were going, etc. No wonder they were taken prisoners. I hope the gentlemen of the press will learn how to be silent about such subjects. There are some things connected with this war which should not be published; it matters not "how bad" the people wish to know them. I am afraid that they will be hung, for the retaliation business has commenced. The Yankees have condemned some of our privateers, and our Governor has selected Col. Cochran and some of his followers to be executed—this is by way of retaliation. This kind of proceeding will make it a dreadful war—a war in which no quarter will be asked or given. I have no hopes for a speedy termination of the war. If it were to last ten years I would not be surprised. I believe that it was necessary for the South to secede, but I think that we will never have much more peace. How can we? The border states are infected and in the course of time will become more so. Missouri and Virginia will both give us trouble, and if Kentucky secedes, she will be ready at any moment to revolt. There may be peace, but it cannot be permanent. I hope I will get an education.

My room-mate is named Mr. Graham. He is from Virginia. The Yankees have been stealing Negroes from the county in which he lives. He was in the Army but got out and came to the University. He is studying law. A great many study medicine because they wish to become surgeons in the Army. General Lee has a son going to school here. The students have organized a military company. Gen. Lee's son is Captain. So I have the opportunity of drilling every evening. I like it very much and it is such good exercise. Gen. Lee has gone to the coast; the Yankees have not attempted to invade S.C. They have taken some parts; but I reckon they will soon be compelled to leave the coast. A dispatch says that our men have determined to neither ask nor give quarter. I hope this is not true, for it increases the horrors of war and deadens the best feelings of the heart.

Where is John White's company? Have they gone to Virginia? I think they ought to go to the Florida coast; they will have more work to do there than in Virginia. The Federal fleet has passed Fernandina. I expect Apalachicola will be attacked. Has the cotton been removed? The Yankees got some cotton in So. Carolina.

I am afraid you will not be able to get enough money for me.

I will need $100.00. Most all the money comes to Virginia. I hope the Government will get out some kind of "medium." Have you seen any Treasury notes? They are used a great deal up here. I reckon the Government will give these notes for cotton. They are small like bank notes, and will do for circulation.

We have no chaplain this session. We have to go to town when we go to church. Love to all. Write soon. Your affectionate son,

JOHN D. PITTMAN

CHAPTER

IX

LIFE AT FROG LEVEL, even in this sad time, went on as usual. The slaves were faithful and devoted, though the older ones realized the uncertainty of their future. Still, crops were planted and harvested, slaughtering was done and meat hung in the smokehouse to cure. Preparations for Christmas were under way when Grandma received a letter from John, which she read to the family:

*University of Virginia,*
*Dec. 4th, 1861*

MY DEAR MOTHER:

I received your kind letter a few days ago. I am always glad to get such long letters. It is no use to write to the Higgs boys at Scotland Neck, N.C., for I reckon they are all in the Army. I have not heard where they are. There are several young men here from N.C. There are a great many from Alabama. I am the only one from Florida. My best friend is Mr. Weeden from Huntsville, Ala. We go to the Presbyterian Church. Dr. Hoge is the best Presbyterian preacher I ever heard. He preached in New York for ten years, but Virginia is his native state and when she seceded he came back to his old home. He delivered a beautiful farewell sermon to the people in New York City the very day the battle of Manassas was fought. He says we look with too much contempt upon the enemy. He thinks this will cause the Southerners to become careless. He says there are a great many brave people at the North; if not there would be no glory in defeating the enemy. My great desire to get an education is the only thing that keeps me from the battlefield.

I intend to go to Richmond next February to see Jeff Davis inaugurated. I am sorry I did not go to Washington to see old

Lincoln put in office. You must write and give me permission to go to Richmond. If you do not, the chairman will not give me a leave of absence.

Love to all. Write soon. Your affectionate son,

JOHN D. PITTMAN

When she finished reading, Pa said, "I guess the boy wouldn't be able to come to us for Christmas; they have such a short holiday and travel is so hard."

"No, Mr. Blackshear, but I thank you for thinking of him," said Grandma. "John will be with his school friends and will enjoy his holiday in Virginia, I am sure."

After the holidays, Grandma told Pa that Mary had completed her schooling in Marianna and was ready for college if he was able to send her. There was much discussion on the subject between Pa, Grandma and Mary, resulting in the decision for Mary to enter Wesleyan Female College in Macon, Georgia, in the fall of 1862.

Mary decided not to return to Marianna with Grandma in February.

"I want to stay with Pa and Ned until I go off to school," was her excuse. Pa and Grandma winked at each other because they knew Cince Guyton, now a young Colonel in the Confederate Army, had much to do with her decision! Cince was home for a few day's leave. Their childhood attachment had ripened into love. The Blackshears and Guytons were great friends and frequent visiting went on between the two families. A marriage between Mary and Cince would be pleasing to both families. Having Mary for the ensuing months as mistress and hostess at Frog Level put a lot of sunshine into Pa's and Ned's life.

One more letter came from John before Grandma left to return to Marianna. The family listened eagerly as she read:

*University of Virginia,*
*January 15th, 1862*

MY DEAR MOTHER;

I received your letter and was delighted to hear from home. I received the book you sent me; it will be of great service to me in reviewing for my examinations. Two of my exams will come off next month. I hope to get through very well. You have to pass the intermediate in order to get a diploma; no one is certain of one until he gets it; a diploma is worth something from this University.

I am glad there is some prospect of getting $150.00. That amount will be sufficient to take me through and leave something besides. Most any Southern bank will do to check. A New Orleans bank would do, or a check upon a Georgia bank. If you can buy a check upon any of the Virginia banks you had better do so.

There is a great deal of sickness about here. One of the students named Norwood, about 17 years old, died very suddenly and unex-pectedly a few days ago. He has 2 brothers here. His father was here when he died. His father is an Episcopal minister. His body was carried to Richmond. They are from Georgetown. They are refugees and cannot go home on account of the Yankees having possession of Georgetown. I suppose his friends will meet and pass a tribute of respect.

The day for the inauguration of Jeff Davis is fast approaching. I will not spend too much money because I know how hard it is to get where I live. Write soon. Your affectionate son,

JOHN D. PITTMAN

# CHAPTER

# X

PA AND MARY were sitting on the front steps one morning after breakfast. Pa spied the blacksmith, "Red-Eyed" Andrew—so-called because one eyeball had been injured and removed—stealthily making his way to the blacksmith's shop.

Pa called to him, "Come here! The way you're sneaking along behind bushes looks to me like you are just now getting to work."

"I is, Marster."

"What do you mean, going so late to work?"

" 'Fo' Gawd, Marster, I'se jes' woke up," explained Andrew.

"That's no excuse! You haven't but one eye, so it should only take half as much sleep for you as it does these other Negroes who get to work at sun-up."

"Dat's jes' it, Marster!" Andrew explained. "I'se got a body lak de rest; I works jes' as hard an' I gits jes' as tired, an' I needs de same amount o' sleep; but I ain't got but one eye to sleep it wid."

"Well, don't let it happen again," said Pa.

Mary turned to Pa with a smile. "Pa, I love the way these Negroes outwit you."

"I do, too," he answered, "but I can't let them know it."

It was April of 1862 when Grandma next visited Frog Level. How glad Pa, Mary and Ned were to see her, and what a warm welcome the servants gave her!

As usual, on the first night, she read John's last two letters to her interested family audience.

*University of Virginia,*
*March 15, 1862*

MY DEAR MOTHER:

These are boisterous times indeed. We don't know one minute what will happen the next. Everything is so uncertain and wavering that I doubt whether I am profiting by remaining at the University.

I don't think there is much to be feared on account of the railroad. If the Yankees take the Wilmington & Weldon R.R. I can go through East Tennessee and Atlanta, Ga., but if they cut off that way also, I can go from here to Lynchburg, Va., from there to Danville. From Danville it is only 40 miles to the railroad at Greensboro, N.C.; from there, there is a railroad that leads to Columbia, S.C., and Augusta, Ga. I could easily hire a private conveyance to go from Danville to Greensboro—so I have 3 ways of getting home. One of them is not likely to be cut off at all. But there is danger from another source. Our Army has fallen back from Manassas to the Rappahannock River. That is a better position than Manassas but there are doubts about our force being able to hold it. A great many of our soldiers are home on furlough; some have failed to re-enlist. Some of the Yankee Army on the Potomac is thoroughly organized. Ours is far from being so. The majority of the people think that our men will make a successful stand, but there are some who doubt it. The question is whether that doubt is enough to make me come home. If our forces are defeated the Yankees will certainly overrun this portion of Virginia. Now, I have a horror of being taken prisoner as a civilian; if I am taken I wish to be taken as a soldier. I cannot hope to complete my education at the University. If I come home I feel it is my duty to go into the Army; sometimes I feel that such is my duty now. If I do go (which is more than probable even if I am permitted to remain here until the end of the session) I hope you will become reconciled to my going. I hope you will not indulge in unnecessary grief. I hope you will commit me to God and believe that what He does is best. Whether I am at home or on the battlefield I am in the midst of death. There are many that will survive the conflict. For your sake more than my own I pray that I may be among that number, but if I fall a sacrifice upon the altar of my country, remember it is the will of God that I die in a glorious cause. This is no time for us to indulge in fears, we must learn to make any sacrifice, even to offer up our lives. I do tell you now that until men quit doubting and coveting and prophesying; that until men cease to hang back from the ranks of those who are opposing the enemy, the South will never pass triumphantly through her peril.

I would like very much to have an office, but if I cannot get one I must go as a private. If I could get a third Lieutenantcy in one of the companies being made up at home I would return without delay, but cannot expect to be chosen above those who are present. If I have to go as a private I will join some well-organized company. I think I could go along as 3rd Lieut. as I have been drilling here in companies of young men.

I wish you would send me up about $20.00 as that would stand in the place of the money I spent by going to Richmond. I tell you to buy a check on Columbus, Ga., bank. I enquired at the bank here and there is no doubt about my being able to sell it. You had better get the check as there will be no danger if I should happen to leave here before it arrives. Love to all. Write soon. Your affectionate son,

JOHN D. PITTMAN

As Grandma folded the letter and took out the second one, she said, "This one came only five days later, Mr. Blackshear."

*University of Virginia,*
*March 21, 1862*

MY DEAR MOTHER:

After mature deliberation I have concluded it is best to come home. I am not learning a great deal at this time; the times are so uncertain that I cannot give my schools proper attention. Also, one of my professors is absent and has been absent for some time. His family lives in Western Virginia and are in danger of being taken by the enemy. There is no telling when he will return.

A great many are of the opinion that Gen. Johnston will throw this place out of his line and if he does there is danger of my not being able to get any baggage from this place. For several weeks there has been no train running to Richmond and the track has been so blocked with cars and supplies that it has been impossible to get any baggage from here to Richmond. People have been compelled to ride a great many miles to a canal in order to get their baggage through to that place. The track is open now but there is no telling when it will be blocked again.

If I had hopes of coming here another session I would desire to

remain. There are a great many things to prevent me from returning. There may not be (it is more than probable) another session.
If I stay until the end of the session I'm afraid I would not be able
to bring any baggage. Students from Mississippi and Arkansas and
Texas are not able to carry any baggage at all. I asked one of my
professors and he seemed to think that if I wished to go South, now
is the time. He did not oppose my going. Another thing, now that
the South is in her greatest danger I feel it my duty to be in the
Army. I would like to join an Artillery Company that will leave
Charlottesville before very long but I know there is probability of
the southern communications being cut off and you would be miserable if you could not hear from me. I would dislike for you to come
up here as it is probable that the greatest of Virginia will be overrun. There is danger of going by Wilmington as the enemy have
taken Newbern and are not far from the railroad. The enemy almost
are marching upon Knoxville and there is not much traveling
through East Tennessee. I will go from here to Richmond and from
there to Weldon and Raleigh, N. C., and on through Columbia,
S. C., to Augusta, Ga. I will not go through Greensboro and Wilmington at all.

I have made the whole plan plain to you. I expect to leave in a
few days. The Secretary of War has exempted the students and
professors of this University from being drafted. There are not
more than 25 students here now; last session we had over 600. I
tell you, the flower of the country is in the Army.

The chairman of the faculty is very much distressed about the
University; the people about here believe that the Yankees will burn
the buildings. What a pity if they do! I expect to be 3 or 4 weeks
getting home. Want to see all my friends before joining the Army.
Love to all. Ever your affectionate son,

JOHN D. PITTMAN

No one spoke as Grandma finished reading this letter. In a
moment, Pa sighed and shook his head. "What decisions the
eighteen- and nineteen-year-old boys are having to make these
days," he said.

"I can only do as he asked, Mr. Blackshear, and commit him
to God."

Grandma's visit was cut short when she heard through a fellow student who returned to Georgia that John would be in Marianna in late May. She was at home to greet him when he arrived.

Grandma wrote Pa that John immediately joined the Confederate Army and was made Sergeant of Company E of the 8th Florida Regiment and that his Company was being sent right away to the fighting arena in Virginia.

Months went by with no word of John, and when the next letter came from Grandma it bore the heartbreaking news that John had been killed. He received a gunshot wound in the great Battle of Manassas on August 30, 1862, and died the next day at Manassas, Virginia—at the age of nineteen years and eight months.

The University Memorial says of John D. Pittman: "It is evident that he possessed literary abilities that would have secured literary distinction in maturer life. At the age of fifteen he was a writer for the papers of Marietta, Georgia, and two years after for the Macon *Telegraph* and the *Field and Fireside*. In October 1860 he became a student at the University of Virginia. He returned the following session and prosecuted his studies until the spring of 1862 when in May he determined to join the army. Going directly home, he volunteered in the "Clark Rifles." This Company was ordered to Tallahassee in June and remained on duty there a month. In July the Rifles—Company E, 8th Florida Infantry, were ordered to the seat of war in Virginia."

CHAPTER

XI

GRANDMA NEVER CEASED to grieve over John's untimely death though she bore her sorrow like a gallant soldier and reconciled herself to "God's will."

Since Grandpa's death, Grandma had continued to live in the Pittman home and run her farms. After John's death her daughter Annie Eliza, wife of Mr. Thomas White, prevailed upon her to bring Becky, her personal servant, and move into the White home. Mr. White managed her farms.

Due to the privations of war and the increased difficulty of travel, Grandma did not get back to Frog Level until the last of May in 1864. Pa and Ned were starved for the sight of her! She made a special effort to get there in time to greet Mary upon her return in June from Wesleyan College to prepare for the homecoming. So she bravely undertook the long journey.

The night she arrived Grandma took out her "specs" and, with tears in her voice, said, "I have only one letter to read tonight. It is my last one from Mary. It tells of a lighter side of college life than we have been reading about." She composed herself and began reading:

*Wesleyan Female College, Macon, Ga.*
*May 4, 1864*

MY DEAR GRANDMA:

Your very interesting letter was received few days ago and I was going to write sooner but waited to see if I couldn't tell you some good news. Well, I can, so here goes!! The Junior places were read out this evening and, would you believe, *my* name was the first one read. Just as soon as my name was read, the girls ran up to me to shower me with flowers, as they do every year when the honors are given out. One of the day-scholars made me a crown of biscuits and threw them over my head. They were strung on a string in the form of a wreath and excited a great deal of laughter. I believe that most of the girls were as rejoiced at my receiving a Junior honor as I was, and such another kissing and congratulating you never did hear of.

You may perhaps be ignorant of the meaning of Junior honor. Well, ten of the best scholars in the class are picked out to read compositions at commencement. You remember I had a Sophomore place last term. Then I had to read a selected piece at night. Now I must read my own composition in the daytime. And the question is *What must I wear?* The Juniors wear white trimmed with blue. I have no white, except tarleton, and do you reckon I'll have to wear that? I never heard of anybody but Mrs. "Gentleman" King wearing tarleton in the daytime, and morning at that! I think I shall attack Pa on that subject this very night. I'm going to tell him, just for fun, that there is "no rose without a thorn" and if he doesn't want to buy a new dress he'd no business to have such a smart daughter! Every girl, I suppose, will have something pretty and I don't want to look worse than any, but I'll not complain as I know times are severe. If Pa consents to give me a dress of some sort of white, you might be able to strike a bargain as you almost always can do. I will write next time about making the dress; I haven't made up my mind.

One of my friends of whom you have heard me speak has run away and married a wild young rascal, one far beneath her in society and everything else. I am grieved to think of her future lot.

Much love to all. I remain your loving grand-daughter,

MARY PITTMAN BLACKSHEAR

No grim thoughts of war seemed to trouble these sweet young girls! What to wear was the problem of the moment—the eternal feminine!

Pa chuckled over Mary's reference to him in the letter. "That girl!" he said, "she really knows how to work her old Pa. Mrs. Pittman, I'd be obliged if you will see that Mary has the dress she will need."

"I'll be glad to, Mr. Blackshear," said Grandma, "Mary's a

good girl and most considerate. I'm sure she would not mention it if it were not important to her. I'll try to find a bargain if possible, Mr. Blackshear."

Pa and Grandma decided to send Ned with the coachman to Macon in the carriage to bring Mary home from Wesleyan in June. He was only twelve years old but a big, overgrown, rosy-cheeked boy, all arms and legs, and suffering the "pangs" and sensitiveness of adolescence. He managed to get himself in and seated alone in the big parlor of Wesleyan. There he waited and waited and waited for Mary! She plotted with her girl friends to precede her into the parlor one by one, to say nothing, but stop and kiss Ned, then silently leave the room. That shy country boy nearly died of embarrassment. He turned red— then white—and by the time Mary appeared to greet him he was pea-green and actively nauseated. She had enjoyed her little joke but her heart melted in repentance at the effect on Ned. She ordered the coachman to drive them downtown to a restaurant because she thought Ned was badly in need of food.

Ned had never been in a restaurant before. In those days it was customary to have a plate of bread already on the tables when diners came in. The waiter came over and asked Ned, "What will you have, Sir?"

Ned looked hopelessly around and said, "I guess I'll have some bread, as I don't see anything else!"

Mary gave his order and the hearty dinner restored his good spirits. He admired the big diamond-shaped gold pin Mary was wearing at her neck. Ned always saw the beautiful. She explained that was her Alpha Delta Phi "society" pin and she prized it highly.

There was a party at Frog Level that night and all the community families came to welcome Mary home. The pinch of war was getting harder, and many families had been saddened by war casualties. Some boys were home on brief leave, others were home recuperating from wounds. Colonel Cince Guyton had managed a two days' leave from his regiment. He and Mary plighted their troth that night and were married next day in the parlor at Frog Level. How sad she was to see him depart to rejoin his regiment!

All of her gay college life was put behind her and she took her place with the other noble women of the South, doing her bit to aid the war effort and keep the home running as smoothly as possible during these terrible days. The slaves were still loyal —they heard much talk about the Yankees but had no clear conception of what a Yankee really was.

It was a late September afternoon in 1864 after Gen. Sherman had sent his army "from Chattanooga, Tennessee through Rossville Gap into Georgia, over-running first Atlanta and then the rest of the state in their fiery 'March to the Sea,' burning everything as they marched." Mary sat on the veranda talking to Ned's old nurse Marthy who was sweeping the porch when she saw smoke in the distance.

Startled, Mary began walking up and down the veranda crying and wringing her hands.

Marthy dropped the broom and ran to her, saying, "What's de m-m-matter, Miss Mary?"

"Oh, Aunt Marthy, the Yankees are coming, the Yankees are coming! I see their smoke!"

" 'Fo' Gawd, Miss Mary," the old darky cried, "is dey g-g-got ch-ch-chimleys to 'em?"

By the grace of God, Sherman's men missed Laurens County.

Neither Grandma nor the Blackshears knew that about the time Sherman and his troops were making their devastating march through Georgia, their beloved Marianna was being raided by General Alexander Asboth—himself a Hungarian adventurer and soldier of fortune—and his Federal troops consisting of one company of deserters, another company of Louisiana Negroes, and the third company of 2nd Maine Cavalry.

It was late October of 1864 when Grandma received the letter from her daughter, Annie White, with newspaper clipping enclosed, telling about the battle at Marianna.

Pa and Mary moved their chairs closer to Grandma so as not to miss a word of news sure to be contained in the letter. As

Grandma settled herself and tore open the envelope, the clipping fell into her lap.

"Mary," she said, "this is such a long letter, suppose you read us the newspaper clipping first so we'll know what it is all about. Your Pa can't see to read it, and your young eyes are better than mine for this fine print."

"All right, I'll be glad to," replied Mary as she reached for the clipping and immediately started reading:

*West Florida News* — EXTRA
*Monday, October 3, 1864*
THE CAPTURE AND SACKING OF MARIANNA AND THE ADJOINING
COUNTIES BY THE YANKEES

It is with feeling of sadness that we are called upon to chronicle the unfortunate fate of our beautiful town which has been within the past week placed in the hands of an unmerciful enemy, the menials of the U.S. Government, in the shape and form of Yankees, deserters and Negroes.

On Friday 23rd ult. news was received here of the capture of a portion of Capt. Chisholm's cavalry company at Eucheeanna, and the advance of the enemy in this direction. On Monday a courier arrived with intelligence that the enemy were near Campbellton, about 18 miles from this place. The military were organized, and two cavalry companies sent to intercept them, who finding the enemy in greatly superior force fell back to our town, where they arrived about 11 o'clock Tuesday morning.

Col. Montgomery, Commandant of the Post, immediately ordered what troops were left here to join the advance and meet the enemy, who appeared on the suburbs of the town about 12 o'clock.

The entire management of the whole affair by the officer commanding our forces is too disgraceful for us to dwell upon it. Suffice it to say, on the approach of the enemy, Col. Montgomery ordered the cavalry to retreat to the bridge across the Chipola, below town, leaving the Home Guards, Captain Norwood (infantry), numbering about fifty men composed of old citizens and boys to defend the town. The Home Guards, finding themselves in this condition, were ordered into the best position the Captain could choose under the circumstances, ranging themselves in line from the residence of Mrs. Ely to the Episcopal Church, with the forces on that street as their protection.

The Yankees, we believe about 600 strong (although acknowledged by officers who are prisoners in our hands to have been between 850 and 1100), advanced slowly, and as they approached within range the gallant and brave little bank of heroes, the Home Guards, opened upon them with their shot guns and whatever arms they had collected from their homes. At the first fire the Adjutant General of the Yankees was killed and some wounded, which caused a panic and the front wheeled and retired in confusion.

The whole force was immediately rallied and with an attempt to cheer them came down the street in full charge two, and in some instances three deep, the Negroes in the rear.

We fought them until finding that we were not supported, resistance being useless on the part of the Home Guards against so overwhelming a force, the order was given by Captain Norwood to fall back immediately farther into town. But it was too late, the enemy had flanked us by sending a force in our rear, passing around the northern position of the town, in the direction of the residence of Judge Wynn in the rear of the Episcopal Church. Our citizens continued to fight them but were finally compelled to surrender, several managing to escape. Most of our killed were butchered and beaten to death after they had surrendered by the infernal Negro troops, who finding them in their power, took the advantage of it. Many who are now spared would have shared the same fate had it not been for intercession on the part of deserters who were formerly acquainted with them

The vandals, having possession of the town, commenced their work of destruction and pillage, bringing destruction, distress and misery to once happy homes. The Episcopal Church, near which our wounded lay, was fired and four bodies burned, two of whom, Mr. John Carter, 6th Florida Regiment (wounded lately in Georgia, and on furlough here), and Mr. Allen, an aged citizen from Greenwood, were only recognized by articles on their persons, or the parts of their bodies not entriely consumed. The residences of Mrs. Hunter and Dr. R. A. Sanders were also burned and the order given to burn the town, but through intercession, was countermanded. The town was completely sacked, everything in the shape of provisions, clothing and valuables that could be carried off, were stolen and havoc pretty generally made.

The Yankees were composed of the 1st and 2nd Maine and the 1st Florida Cavalry (deserters and Negroes). They remained here until two o'clock Tuesday night when they left quietly and speedily, fearing that we would receive reinforcements.

They took Dr. H. Ely, Mr. Wm. Nichols, and several other citizens prisoners and paroled them. The number of Negroes taken from this county is estimated at about 400. Our loss is 9 killed, 16 wounded and 54 prisoners. The Yankee loss is estimated at about 15 killed and 40 wounded. The enemy carried off all their wounded except 6, who are now at the hospitals. Major Cutler and Lieut. Adams, 1st and 2nd Maine Cavalry, are at the residence of Mr. Thos. M. White. Gen. Asboth (Hungarian), who was in command of the expedition, was wounded in three places severely but was carried off when they left. They also lost their Adjutant General, killed in front of Mrs. Ely's gate at the first fire from the Home Guards. Several lieutenants were also wounded. Col. Montgomery commanding our forces is a prisoner in the hands of the enemy. Capt. H. O. Bassett, 6th Florida Regiment, who was here on sick furlough and who went into the action, was wounded and bayoneted and beaten to death with the butts of guns by Negroes and the body so mutilated as to be scarcely recognizable.

It was observed that among the Yankees were two deserters, well known to our citizens and formerly of this place. There were others recognized but we have been unable to obtain their names.

On Wednesday evening last several companies of cavalry under Colonel Scott of the 5th Florida Battalion when in pursuit of the Yankees who were scourging the counties between this and the Gulf but were unable to overtake them, they having reached their transports and gone back to Pensacola several hours before his advance guard got to Point Washington.

For the last few days reinforcements have been arriving from Gadsden and Leon counties, but it is too late. The Yankees stated before they left that they would visit this place again shortly. We hope to be better prepared for them next time. There are some incriminating reports in circulation relative to one of our citizens now with the enemy, but as there seems to be some doubt we refrain from noticing it until it is ascertained to be certain.

Very fortunately our printing office was not very materially damaged. Nearly all the printing paper we had on hand was destroyed and the regular issue of the *News* must necessarily be short or in a more condensed form until we are able to get another supply.

Grandma was sobbing before Mary, with tears in her eyes and a quiver in her voice, came to the end.

"God have mercy on our friends and loved ones and bring comfort to their broken hearts," prayed Grandma. "Here, honey," she said to Mary, "you better read your Aunt Annie's letter to us. I'm too broken up."

"I'll try," said Mary. Taking a tight grip on her own emotions, she read:

*Marianna, Florida,*
*October 20th, 1864*

MY DEAR MA:

It grieves me to send you such bad news. My heart is sad within me.

In the beginning I must say that though Mr. White turned our home into a hospital for the Yankee wounded, I left him and his Negroes to look after them and took myself into the homes where our Confederate sick and wounded were hospitalized. I am glad you are not here to witness the great disaster that has befallen us. Our friends and neighbors are severely criticizing Mr. White for taking in the enemy. They are saying that he, being the richest man in the County, did it to save his property and other valuables. I would like to believe otherwise but I do not understand it; only God knows what his motive was. There has been no doubt or question as to my loyalty.

I shall endeavor to tell you what the newspaper clipping left out.

As you know, Col. Montgomery's headquarters were located in Marianna but he was in command of the Confederate Army from the Apalachicola River in the east to the Chocktawatchee River in the west, and from the southern Alabama line to St. Andrews Bay. His entire force consisted of five small, undisciplined and poorly armed cavalry companies. These companies, with the exception of a

handful of men and horses which he retained in Marianna, were sta-
tioned at various points near St. Andrews Bay to defend the Salt
Works there and to keep watch on the Federal vessels in that part of
the Gulf.

Only old men and young boys, too old or too young to join the
Army, were left in Marianna. All of our strong men capable of
bearing arms were with Lee's Army in Virginia or in the west with
Johnson. There were six or eight soldiers here to recuperate from
wounds received in previous battles. They forgot their wounds and
fought valiantly on our side; some of them were killed.

The two companies of cavalry spoken of in the newspaper were
composed mostly of old men and boys who had horses and could
ride. The hospitals spoken of were private homes converted into
hospitals.

A young man born and reared in the community turned traitor,
deserted his home, family and friends, went to Pensacola, joined
the enemy forces at Barrancas and piloted them to his home county.

On September 26th pickets reported to Col. Montgomery that
the Yankees were coming by way of Campbellton or Vernon. A
company of Home Guards was hastily organized from the town and
surrounding settlements, consisting of boys under 16 and old men
from 50 to 75 years old. They armed themselves with their home
shotguns, old flintlock guns and pistols. None had had any previous
military training—not even Jesse Norwood who was put in command.

In the early morning of September 27th Col. Montgomery received word that the enemy was within 10 miles of Marianna on the
Campbellton Road. He ordered Norwood's Home Guards placed
on active duty in the western part of town. Between the Episcopal
Church and cemetery and Mrs. Hunter's boarding house on the opposite side of Main Street, he ordered a barricade of old wagons and
carts thrown up across the 75 ft. wide street. Behind these and in
the church building he posted Norwood's Home Guards.

Col. Montgomery and his handful of cavalry rode out on the
Campbellton Road and met the enemy about noon. When he saw
how far outnumbered his forces were he ordered a hasty retreat
which never stopped until his remaining men had crossed the
Chipola river bridge and burned it behind them, thus disgracefully
deserting the Home Guards and the town. Col. Montgomery was
captured before he crossed the river. It is whispered the capture was

by pre-arrangement, and he was taken to our home where Maj. Cutler, Lieut. Adams and other Yankee wounded were.

Our old men and boys did not have a chance since Gen. Asboth, having that native deserter to guide him, had sent part of his forces around the town by the road leading to Mrs. Whitehead's place, thence into Main Street below our barricade thus enabling them to also attack from the rear. Gen Asboth had already ordered his Negro troops to set fire to the church and to Mrs. Hunter's boarding house. A merciless slaughter of the Home Guards followed. Those in the cemetery and in the church who attempted to escape were pushed back by the brutal Louisiana Negroes on the point of their bayonets into the burning church, to be burned to cinders.

The ladies in the Hunter house fled for their lives to escape these brutes of Federal soldiers. A lady with her three-day-old infant was miraculously saved after having been thrown from a window on a mattress. Other horrible scenes and incidents could be related but they are too revolting to write about.

Those of the little Spartan band of Confederates not killed or wounded or escaped were carried off as prisoners.

A few hours after the bridge was burned, Major Milton and Capt. Jeter arrived with their cavalry companies. Coming from the St. Andrews Bay region, they came up on the east bank of the river but there was no bridge left to cross over. A messenger swam the river to reach the telegraph office where he wired Major Milton's order to Tallahassee for reinforcements. The telegraph operator, to save his skin, turned traitor and gave Asboth a copy of that message, thus enabling the enemy to retreat hastily during the night, carrying with them all of the horses, wagons, carts, household goods and valuables that they could lay their hands on and induced a number of Negro women to accompany them. The Federal dead were buried without coffins and in such shallow graves that in many instances their hands and feet were left sticking out. They were later taken up by our citizens and buried in the old town graveyard. Twenty-six of the enemy were killed and about 50 wounded. Though General Asboth was wounded, his men, fearing to leave him in Marianna, carried him on their hasty retreat via the shortest cut to Pensacola. More than 50 boys and gray-haired men were killed or burned. The only white person who voluntarily went off with the enemy was our degenerate telegraph operator.

Two days later Gen. W. W. Scott arrived with reinforcements

but it was too late; the enemy reached Ft. Barrancas in safety. The resistance of our little band of Home Guards foiled Gen. Asboth's entire plan. Had he succeeded in destroying the Salt Works and capturing our cavalry he would have dealt the Confederacy a serious blow.

Among the Federal wounded was one gentlemanly cavalry officer, Maj. Nathan Cutler of the 2nd Maine, who is still recuperating at our home. Except for his intervention and protests the atrocities would have been even worse.

In every home we weep for our dead and bind up the wounds of our survivors. In this terrible war there have been battles of greater magnitude and historical importance than the battle of Marianna, but there have been no braver instances of individual heroism or personal courage. Pages of human history, modern and ancient, do not chronicle a more sublime exhibition of human valor. May God bless those who fought and died defending their homes, their families and their friends.

We have had no news from you all since Sherman marched and burned his way through Georgia. I pray he did not go through Laurens County. Give my love to Mr. Blackshear, Mary and Ned. Your loving daughter,

ANNIE ELIZA WHITE

Grandma was shaking with sobs long before the letter ended. Mary embraced her and they wept together. Tears dimmed the fire of wrath and indignation in Pa's eyes.

With a deep sigh, he told them, "There seems to be scarcely a star of hope in the sky. Our armies are depleted and shattered, torn and bleeding. Our principal cities are in the hands of the enemy and the greater portion of our Southland desolated and destroyed beneath the iron tread of the Federal armies."

"Mr. Blackshear," said Grandma, "it seems more than I can stand that our beautiful town of Marianna should undergo such suffering. I was needed there to help care for the wounded."

"Now, Mrs. Pittman, you must not torture yourself with that regret. You are needed here, too, and besides, no one could foresee such a catastrophe. Marianna being remote from the coast and the lines of travel and transportation seemed more secure from the inroads of the enemy than almost any other portion of the Confederacy."

Mary, with the confidence of youth in love, said, "I wish my Cince and his men had been there, then the battle would have had an entirely different ending!"

Though their hearts were heavy, Pa and Grandma could not help but smile at Mary's confidence in her young man.

By 1864 Pa was nearly blind from cataracts and seldom left the plantation. Ned went on all of his business errands with letters explaining the nature of the business. Ned was about fourteen years old when Pa sent him to Savannah, Georgia, to transact business with his cousin, Marmaduke Hamilton. The first night Ned was there, Cousin Duke took him for his first visit to the theater to see Joe Jefferson play Rip Van Winkle.

Ned was entranced with the play. When Rip awakened to a world strange to him after his twenty-year sleep, Ned jumped up out of his seat and said in his loud voice, "Cousin Duke, why doesn't somebody tell him that is his wife?"

After the performance, one of Cousin Duke's Savannah friends touched him on the shoulder and said, "Duke, I enjoyed the play, but I enjoyed your young friend more."

When Ned was sixteen he became infatuated with a woman ten years his senior and not his social equal. Pa called Ned "on the carpet" about the unsuitability of such a situation and acquainted Ned with the "facts of life."

The next week Pa removed the temptation by sending Ned to Marianna to live a while with his Aunt Annie and Uncle Tom White and Grandma, who now lived with her daughter and son-in-law.

Before Ned left, Mary and Cince left Norwood, their plantation, and moved to Frog Level so Mary could look after her nearly blind Pa, and Cince operated his own and Pa's plantations.

In Marianna, Ned's first formal schooling began. Heretofore

he had been taught at home. He was a handsome boy, six feet two inches tall, and he seemed all arms and legs.

The first Friday afternoon in school, to his amazement, the teacher called on every boy and girl for a declamation or recitation. Ned wasn't prepared but he closely observed the boys and girls as they walked to the platform and said their speech.

When the teacher called "Ned Blackshear," he unfolded his length, strode to the platform, bowed low and from the waist and said in a loud voice, "The sea-tick bit off the red-bug's toe, and the red-bug hollered Oh, God, oh!" He bowed again and took his seat. Judging by the mirth of the teacher and pupils Ned presumed he had made a great speech.

Youth adjusts quickly and it wasn't long before he was "one of the boys" and as much at home in the schoolroom as the others were. With his sweet and fun-loving disposition, he made friends easily.

The next year he noticed a lovely little girl who had just entered school. This was Major Milton's daughter Belle. She was as beautiful and dainty as a fairy princess. She had a mass of curls, shading in color from gold to chestnut brown. So thick were they that they bounced all over her shoulders as she ran about the school grounds where the sunlight brought out the many shades of gold and brown. She was then just a little girl, but Ned noticed her because she was so beautiful.

At twenty, Ned's school days came to an end when he received word that Pa had passed away. Ned was deeply grieved, and seemed to "grow up" overnight. He felt it was time for him to quit school and go to work and take his place as a man in the world.

Ned conveyed his part of the plantation to his sister Mary, and she and Cince continued to live at Frog Level. Ned stayed in Marianna and went to work for his uncle, Tom White, in his mercantile store.

Youth rebounds quickly from sorrow, and Ned was soon a gay and carefree "blade" around town. His personality was dynamic and electrifying. No party was ever dull if he attended.

His violin playing, accompanied on the piano by his cousin Eliza Kellam, was greatly enjoyed. He and Cousin Eliza gave generously of their talents to all public entertainments as well as to private parties.

Ned was very popular. He squired the girls around and hunted, fished and played poker with the men—his frank, open countenance did not make his poker playing very profitable!

In Aunt Annie's back yard he kept and trained his bird dogs and their puppies. One day he came in and found Aunt Annie in tears.

"Why, Auntie, what is the matter?" he asked.

"One of your puppies got into the house, found my Sunday bonnet and tore it up!" she said with a sob.

Ned, relieved that it was nothing more serious, put his arms around her, kissed her and said, "Auntie, please excuse him. He didn't know it was your *Sunday* bonnet!"

Thus her good humor was restored.

Mr. Quarterman, the Presbyterian minister who lived in DeFuniak, also preached at Auntie's church in Marianna. She looked forward to entertaining her beloved pastor on his visits to her church. On the Sundays he was expected she would have Mandy prepare all the things he liked best to eat.

One mid-week morning Mr. Quarterman showed up unexpectedly. Aunt Annie was happy to see him but she was in a panic about how Mandy could prepare him a good dinner on such short notice.

With the greeting over, Auntie rushed to the back porch and called Mandy to the walkway between the kitchen and back porch. The roof of the kitchen and roof did not join; there was a space of four feet between them.

"Mandy, Mr. Quarterman will be here for dinner. What can we have that will be good?"

As they stood talking a covey of frightened partridges flew between the two roofs, and eight of them hit the eaves and fell at their feet.

Old Mandy stooped down, picked up the quail, put them in

her outstretched apron and said, "Miss Annie, de Lawd done sent de preacher his dinner."

After the quail dinner had been enjoyed, Auntie and Mr. Quarterman were talking in the parlor.

"Mr. Quarterman," Auntie said, "I'm glad you came today because I've been troubled. At times I do not feel close to God and I'm just not satisfied about my Christian life."

Mr. Quarterman smiled. "Well, cheer up, Mrs. White," he said, reassuringly, "if you were entirely satisfied about yourself I should feel very uneasy about you."

# XIII

WHILE NED WAS WORKING for Uncle Tom, his beloved Grandma passed to her reward. This was Ned's greatest sorrow. He missed her so much he wanted to get away from the home, so he told Uncle Tom he had been offered the managership of the Neal's Landing warehouse and he had decided to take it. This was a responsible position since all county freight, merchandise, cotton, naval stores and other farm products as well as passengers were shipped on the picturesque steamboats to Columbus, Georgia, and Apalachicola, Florida, to be reloaded there for their final destination.

The manager's quarters were in the rear of the warehouse. Ned liked the day-time hustle and bustle of activity, but at night—after the steamers had been loaded and passed on their way, and the farmers and merchants, having collected their wares, loaded their wagons and returned to their homes—this was a lonesome job. Ned, like Uncle Reuben, always wanted "somebody." He was no lover of solitude. He did not like the eerie feeling of loneliness at night. Determined to overcome it, he stayed on two years at Neal's Landing.

Finally came one stormy afternoon when old man Ricks' body was brought in his coffin to be stored until the steamboat was due two days later. The Negroes who had brought the body left; darkness came; the storm grew in intensity—lightning, thunder and pouring rain. All Ned could think of was being alone with old man Ricks' body! All the Negro superstitions he had absorbed asserted themselves; his spine tingled, his hair stood on end. When he twisted and turned on his bed the creak-

ing springs said "Ricks! Ricks!" Said Ned to himself, "I'll go
out in the storm to be rid of that dead man."

He dressed and as he started out the key turning in the lock
seemed to say "Ricks!" The turn of the doorknob said "Ricks!"
Outside he breathed easier until he became drenched with rain
and his shoes filled with water. Then every step he took, his
water-soaked shoes squeaked "Ricks! Ricks! Ricks! Ricks!"

Never was Ned so glad to see daylight and to hear wagons
and carriages rolling in with freight and people! He resigned
that day as manager of the warehouse. He hired two Negroes to
sleep on pallets in the warehouse until a new manager could
relieve him.

Auntie, Uncle Tom and "little Annie"—who was growing
into a young lady by now—were overjoyed to see Ned, and all
the servants were pleased that he was back. Even old Mandy
prepared his favorite dishes for his first breakfast at home. When
she brought in a heaping plate of hot battercakes, Ned, mischief
dancing in his eyes, took only one cake. Mandy just stood there
holding the cakes as she cajolingly said, "Take 'nother un, honey,
t' keep t' other un hot."

Ned laughed and said, "Now I know I'm home after hearing Mandy say that." And he served himself bountifully with
the steaming golden cakes.

"Well, Ned," said Uncle Tom, "what are your plans?"

"Nothing too definite, Sir, but I think I'd like to have a
business of some kind. I've saved a little money from my warehouse job and thought I'd try to invest it that way," Ned replied. "I'd like your advice on it, Uncle Tom."

"Do you think you'd like to run a livery stable?"

"That wouldn't be bad at all, Uncle Tom. I believe I could
do real well with one." Ned's interest was plain to see. "How did
you ever think of that for me?"

"Well, old man Johns who ran the stable near the square
died while you were away. He had no boys to leave the business
to, and his widow wants to see the place sold. I was hoping you'd
get back before she sold it, because I thought it would interest
you."

Livery stables were a lucrative business in those days. All the drummers who came to town on the train hired a vehicle and horses to make their rounds to outlying stores in their territory and to carry their trunks of samples. The young men hired horses and buggies to take their young ladies for an afternoon drive, and riding horses, too, were greatly in demand.

Ned bought the stable and thus was launched on a business venture of his own. He loved every minute of it because there were always people around besides the colored men who looked after the horses and other equipment and did all the menial chores.

CHAPTER

# XIV

NED'S BUSINESS prospered and he led a happy life. He joined the
Sportsman's Club and enjoyed the hunting and fishing every
chance he had. The woodlands abounded in game of all sorts—
these men could never imagine that game would ever be scarce—
and there were no "posted" fields. When a hunt was over, there
was a game supper given in the town hall to which the entire
community was invited. When the men returned from fishing
trips to nearby lakes they would have a community fish fry.
These events were eagerly looked forward to.

Ned was popular with young and old alike, and especially
the young ladies. On his birthday two of them each sent him a
chocolate cake, and had the cakes delivered at the livery stable.
Gallant that he was, and happy to be remembered, Ned showed
no partiality—he rested one foot on a buggy step and, without
stopping, ate *both* cakes. Needless to say, he never again liked
chocolate in any form!

His attentions to one of the not-so-young ladies was miscon-
strued. She read into it more ardor than he felt or intended, and
when Ned perceived that she was heading him toward a marriage for which he had no enthusiasm, he sought a gentlemanly
way out.

He confided his problem to Uncle Tom and Aunt Annie
and asked that they not let young Annie know anything about
it as he did not wish it discussed in her young set. He wished to
protect the not-so-young lady involved.

Wise Uncle Tom said, "You better go to Georgia for a visit with Mary and Cince until this blows over."

"I can't leave my business for that length of time."

"I will buy your business for what you have invested, Ned. With the good help you have there I'll continue to run the business for myself, and when you return I'll sell it back to you at the same price I pay for it."

"That is fine, Uncle Tom. I can get a job in Dublin without being worried about what is happening to my business here."

Mary and Cince were happy to see Ned and he was glad to be with them. Mary was not well. She was suffering from malaria —chills and fever, they called it then—so prevalent in those days when houses were not screened against flies and mosquitoes. Quinine was their only remedy to combat this dreaded disease.

Ned enjoyed several days resting and visiting with Mary and Cince. He missed and mused upon the old way of life at Frog Level during his boyhood days when Pa and the beloved slaves were there and when Grandma came for those wonderful long visits.

Mary and Cince were glad when he told them he was going to stay close by for a while if he could find a good job in Dublin. Cince had a horse saddled for Ned and he rode into Dublin where he secured employment at Lanier's mercantile store. He got room and board with a nice family and was more or less happy. He had some old friends there and made many new ones.

Though he entered into all the social life of the town, he had many homesick moments. Too much of Marianna was woven into his life. Aunt Annie had been and was still like a mother to him. He had great respect and high regard for Uncle Tom, and he loved Annie like a little sister. Theirs was the only real home he'd ever known. He knew that eventually he would go back, but he hated to leave as long as Mary's health was so bad. Then, too, he was still getting an occasional letter from the not-so-young lady in Marianna.

In the second year of his sojourn in Georgia he received the following "business" letter from Uncle Tom:

*Marianna, Fla.*
*Aug. 15, 1880*

DEAR NED,

My livery stable is up for sale. Would you be interested in buying?

Sincerely,
UNCLE TOM

P.S. A certain young lady was married yesterday to the new Baptist minister.

Ned ran out of Lanier's store and immediately dispatched this telegram to Uncle Tom:

Hold the deal. I am buying. Be home soon. Ned.
P.S. Halleluiah.

Ned made arrangements to hire one of his friends to take his place in Lanier's store, but his exuberant plans for immediate return to Florida were sadly delayed another thirty days by the death of his dear sister Mary. He felt very much alone with Mary gone. He had no Blackshear kin nearer than first cousins, though he loved these cousins devotedly, especially Tom who had been like a brother to him during their boyhood days. Now he had no Pittman kin except Aunt Annie and little Annie, and he realized how fortunate he was to have a home with them and Uncle Tom. Though pressure was brought to bear on him to remain in Laurens County, he followed the dictates of his heart and returned to Marianna.

Ned was pleased and touched by the warm welcome from family, friends and servants. He bought back his business from Uncle Tom and life went on much as it had before. He called on the young ladies, took them driving, squired them to entertainments, played his violin with Cousin Eliza's accompaniment, sang in the church choir, and scattered sunshine and kindness as he went his way.

The following spring, Annie, who now had graduated from college in Stanton, Virginia, said, "Ned, I'm going to have a party tonight for Belle Milton who returned yesterday from

Slade College in Columbus and I expect you to be here."

Belle had gone away to school soon after Ned went to work at Neal's Landing so he had not seen her for several years.

"Don't tell me that beautiful child has grown into a young lady!" said Ned.

Annie, with an indignant toss of her head, said, "She certainly has, and if you paid more attention to me and my friends instead of those older girls you'd have realized that we are grown up."

Ned smiled and said, "Get that pout off your pretty face; I'll come to your party. May be a little late but I'll be there to give you and Belle a whirl in the dance."

When Ned arrived home that night the guests were arriving, so he slipped up the back stairs to his room to get dressed for the party. As he descended the front stairs to join the merrymakers, his eyes fell upon Belle dancing with her escort, Mr. Vealie.

She was a vision of loveliness wearing a low-necked, sleeveless blue satin bodice which came to a point in back and front over a very full white *point d'esprit* skirt with full taffeta petticoats beneath it. Her lovely bronze curls were done in a French twist, brought to the top of her head, coiled and secured with hairpins. The ends were curled and spilled over to one side and back.

Ned was spellbound! Her little 5'2" figure was perfect in that well-fitted dress, and how her little feet could dance! When the music ceased he made his way to her.

With a courtly bow, he said, "Miss Belle, may I have the next dance?"

"Yes, Mr. Blackshear. It is nice to see you again."

From then on he claimed as many dances as she would allow. Before the evening was over he knew that, despite the eight years' difference in their ages, she was the only girl in the world for him. His courtship started as he danced with her that night in the spacious hall of Aunt Annie's home.

Belle, too, felt a new awakening in her heart, evidenced by a warmer flush on her face and a new sparkle in her eyes.

Next morning at breakfast Ned told Annie again how much he enjoyed her party, and he asked many questions about Belle.

"You seem very interested in the younger set all of a sudden!"

I am," he replied, "because I think Miss Belle is going to be my wife."

"Don't get your hopes up too high," Annie warned, "because Mr. Vealie, the school principal, is very attentive to her. He escorted her to the party last night."

"Is Miss Belle in love with him?"

"Now that I cannot tell you, but everyone thinks that will be a match. Mrs. Milton, Belle's mother, looks favorably upon Mr. Vealie as a suitor for Belle's hand."

Ned did not let this news deter him. He had always been a welcome visitor in Major Milton's home, but now he began to call on the family more frequently. He realized his would be a rugged courtship because Mrs. Milton so strongly favored Mr. Vealie. The odds were against Ned, because in those days daughters were dutiful, and it was unheard of to defy one's mother.

Ned had a staunch ally in Belle's young sister Berta. She went to school to Mr. Vealie and she was not fond of him. She much preferred "Mr. Blackshear" because he always noticed her and paid her compliments and he was fun to be with. She would sit on the joggling-board in the front yard and wait for him to stop by. She would then inform him, as best she knew, of the progress of Mr. Vealie's courtship.

It was really a hot race between the two suitors! Belle wouldn't consent to marry Mr. Vealie and she wouldn't go against her mother's wishes and consent to marry Ned. This state of affairs continued for two and a half years.

Belle's older sister, Susie, was married to a promising young man—destined to be Governor of Georgia for two terms—William Yates Atkinson, and they lived at his home in Newnan, Georgia. Susie was a lovely lady, very smart and ambitious—not the sentimental type. She was a great help to Mr. Atkinson during his political career. Their son, William Yates, Jr., many years later was Acting Chief Justice on the Georgia Supreme Court. Another son, Bert Milton, was a flier in the unsafe crates our boys flew in World War I. He was a close friend of Billy Mitchell and was the "silent partner" with Billy Mitchell in his fight for better planes and more recognition for the Air Force as an important part of our armed forces. Susie's youngest child was born in the Governor's mansion in Atlanta, and they named her Georgia.

Susie came home occasionally on a visit. This time her mother had summoned her "to help Belle make up her mind to marry Mr. Vealie." Mr. Vealie was well educated and shrewd in the ways of making money. Mr. Blackshear, she said, was a "charming man, but the happy-go-lucky type who would never amount to anything in the financial world." Susie obeyed her mother's wishes, but she didn't try too much persuasion on Belle because Susie herself thought a great deal of Ned and greatly enjoyed his company.

While Susie was visiting her old home, a much beloved old lady in town passed away. The old lady had been confined for years to a wheelchair, and her limbs were badly drawn from rheumatism—so badly drawn, in fact, that to straighten them it was necessary to strap her chest and knees to the "cooling board" on which she was laid out before the funeral.

It was customary in those days for friends to sit up all night with the dead. Ned and Belle had both volunteered to "sit up." Mrs. Milton deemed this arrangement highly improper because Ned was "paying court" to Belle, so she sent Susie to take Belle's place. Ned, though disappointed, was glad to see Susie and to have her good company.

As Ned and Susie sat in the room with the corpse, conversing in low tones as the clock ticked nearer to daylight, the chest strap on the body broke and the corpse sprang to a sitting position. Ned afterwards said, "Susie and I didn't stop running until day-after-tomorrow!"

CHAPTER

# X V

SEVERAL MONTHS AFTER SUSIE'S return to Newnan, Mrs. Milton
became ill. When a month had passed and she was no better,
Major Milton became alarmed. Thinking a higher climate would
be beneficial and that the skill of Atlanta doctors could cure
her malady, he sent Belle with her mother to Susie's home in
Newnan, Georgia. But, alas, her disease was incurable, and she
passed away at her daughter's home.

Ned realized how sad and tender Belle's heart would be
toward her mother's memory, and he felt that his "suit" was
lost because Belle would not now go against her mother's expressed wish. He called at the home to express his sympathy to
Major Milton and the family, and asked Major Milton to convey
his sympathy to "Miss Belle."

Upon Belle's return to Marianna, Ned left the "field" wide
open to his rival. He did not ask to call, but how he suffered for
the sight of her and his longing to be with her. He honestly
thought it would be easier for Belle if he stayed away.

After about six restless, agonizing weeks of this, he found
himself at twilight one afternoon walking by the Milton home,
hoping to catch a distant glimpse of Belle. When he reached the
gate it was open, and Belle was sitting alone on the top front
step.

Mastered by his overwhelming desire, he almost ran up the
walk and steps to speak to her. She looked up at him, eyes brimming with tears, and said, "So you came at last."

"My little Belle," he said, as he took her in his arms, and
they poured out their love and longing for each other.

From that moment he knew she was his and he was the happiest man in the world. He spoke to Major Milton for her hand in marriage after a suitable period of mourning had passed.

They had a beautiful wedding in historic St. Luke's Episcopal Church in Marianna on the night of December 6, 1883. The solemnity of the occasion was almost wrecked, however, by Jim Dixon, the best man, when, as Ned was slipping the wide yellow gold wedding band—inscribed "To My Little Belle"—on the bride's finger and repeating after the rector "with all my worldly goods I thee endow," Jim stage-whispered "goodby collars and cuffs!"

The reception at the Milton home was festive and gay. One of the guests said, "Ned, you married the nicest girl in town, but you remained a bachelor too long. You'll never live to see your children grown."

How wrong he was! Fifty-two years later, Ned held his great-grandson upon his knee!

After the good nights were said and the last guest had departed, Belle and Ned finally reached the seclusion of their bedroom in Aunt Annie's home, where they were to reside for a few months. The door was scarcely closed and Ned took Belle into his arms, when from the street came cries of "Fire! Fire! Fire!"

They rushed to look out of the window and saw flames leaping from one of the stores. Those were the days of the "bucket brigade" when every man was self-appointed to lend his strength to help extinguish every fire. With a quick kiss for his bride, Ned rushed out to join the fire fighters.

It was a bitter cold night; the wind was blowing and many of the stores were built of wood, so their desperate efforts were in vain. The flames spread and nearly every business house in Marianna was burned down that night. Ned's livery stable and several of his horses were destroyed. When it was all over and Ned had time to reflect, he said, "I know I'm the only man in the world who ever fought fire all night long on his wedding night"

After the fire, Ned went into the mercantile business, and

Belle taught school a few years. Major Milton gave them a home near his own for a wedding present. Here they lived for thirteen years. Three boys and one girl blessed their union. Their first son, Milton, died at twenty-two months old; the second son, Edward, died when he was nine years old. Belle was so grieved that Ned decided a change of residence would be beneficial, so he and Belle with their two younger children, Will and Rita, left their Marianna home and moved to Dublin, Georgia.

Back in his native town, Ned bought a home, hired Rosa to cook for Belle, and went into the insurance business.

CHAPTER

# XVI

AT THE AGE of forty-three Ned was a handsome and distinguished-looking man. His 215 pounds were well distributed over his 6'2" frame. He had beautiful deep-blue eyes, a large well-shaped nose, generous mouth with full top lip on which he wore a close-cropped mustache. His ever-ready laughter was hearty and infectious, loud but not boisterous, and he still possessed a magnetic personality. His appearance at any gathering electrified those present and awakened new interest. He never failed to be entertaining. His kindness was unbounded and his deep love for humanity was beyond description. He had the soul of a musician, the "call" of a minister and the mischievousness of Puck. He was the ridiculous and the sublime, yet these contradictions in character were in perfect balance. Only the good and the beautiful appealed to him. He was ever trying to better mankind and sowing seeds of character in the youthful. While his heart was deeply religious, his eyes twinkled with devilment. He was gay or sad as the occasion demanded. His life was like a lively symphony accompanied by the pathos of minor chords.

Belle at thirty-five was the quintessence of elegance in every respect. Her hazel eyes were set wide apart under a beautiful brow crowned with thick curly hair now worn parted in the middle, waved on the sides and piled high on top of her head in a Psyche knot. A little curl escaped on each side at the nape of her neck. She was human beauty at its perfection. Ned said, "When God made Belle He must have rested three days to admire His handiwork." Though small in stature she had the dignity, graciousness and regal bearing of royalty; the pride of

Lucifer and a delightful sense of humor that tided her over many
rough places.

In their home she was truly a queen. Her realm was not one
of wealth, but her family subjects daily laid their gifts of love
at her feet. She ruled with a scepter of love, wisdom and justice.
She had but one weakness—her son Will—but who could blame
her for that? Having lost her two older boys, she could never
believe that Will was physically strong. She petted, pampered
and over-indulged him. She was his "shock absorber," standing
between him and every unpleasant experience in life. Consequently, and tragically, he never reached man's full estate in
strength of character or self-mastery. He was easily influenced
by those present at the moment. He was a lovable boy; a gentleman with courtly manners, ready wit and a master at repartee.
Whiskey and women were his greatest weaknesses and proved to
be his final undoing. Even that tragedy and heartbreak for those
who loved him had its humorous side.

Ned and Belle were prominent and active in all social, political, civic and church affairs in Dublin. There was always a welcome in their home for friends or strangers. People liked to come
there where they found love, music and good fellowship.

Ned never turned a deaf ear to the many Negroes who
knocked at his back door seeking advice and guidance. They laid
their troubles on "Mr. Ned's" shoulders, secure in the knowledge
that he would, so far as was within his power, see that they received just treatment.

Ned made a good living because it was necessary, but he had
no desire to accumulate wealth. Life to him was a great adven-
ture, to be lived fully and abundantly. Their home in Dublin is
most aptly described by a line from an old song—"Not much
money but, oh, my honey, ain't we got fun!"

Ned and Belle often entertained friends at home. Few such
evenings were planned—people "just came." One of the most
welcome guests was "Miss Ann," organist and choir director at
the Methodist Church. Ned sang bass in her choir, and they had
become great friends. She was an accomplished musician and was
much in demand at all community affairs and private parties.

She and Ned were kindred spirits, sharing the same keen sense of the ridiculous and love of music and of entertaining.

To celebrate their first Christmas in their new home, Ned and Belle gave an eggnog party for their many friends. Miss Ann at the piano accompanied Ned on his violin. The music was gay, the crowd in a jovial, holiday mood.

Belle put all the "fixings" for the eggnog on the big round dining table and, under her supervision, the guests took turns beating the eggs and whipping the cream. The huge double sliding doors between the front room and parlor and between parlor and dining room were opened wide, making one large L-shaped room for the festive crowd. The eggnog bowl, used solely for that purpose, was heavy crockery twenty-four inches in diameter and a good eight-inches deep, and when the beaters were finished and the bowl was brimming with the creamy yellow nog, Belle served the big glasses.

"I swear," said Ned, bringing his glass back for a refill, "I believe Belle makes better eggnog every time."

In the course of the evening, Ned consumed four glasses of eggnog and started back to the bowl for another. Belle touched his sleeve and whispered, "Mr. Blackshear, there isn't any more."

Ned's booming voice rang out for all to hear. "My God, Belle, when you make eggnog, why don't you *make* eggnog!"

And his hearty laughter joined that of his guests.

When the last guest had departed, Ned banked the fires in the grates, locked the doors and turned out the lights while Belle went in to see about the children. Rosa, the cook, would clean up in the morning before breakfast.

Ned was already in his long white nightshirt when Belle came in. Sitting in his chair by the open fire they talked over the evening while Belle got ready for bed. Ned never tired of seeing her brush her beautiful long hair and plait it in two thick braids which ended in a curl. He constantly marveled that she had, somehow, chosen him.

The braids finished, Belle said, "It's late, Mr. Blackshear. Better bank the fire and put out the light."

Ned said good night and soon was sleeping peacefully. A few

hours later, though it seemed like minutes, they were awakened by the fire alarm. In those days, the whole town turned out for a fire, day or night, and since Ned was in the insurance business he felt doubly bound to be there and was usually one of the first to arrive.

Sleepily, he bounded out of bed and, to his dismay, discovered with his bare foot that Will's puppy had visited his room and left his "card," unnoticed until that moment.

"My God, Belle," he shouted, "bring me a pan of water!"

Belle, ever the dutiful wife, brought the water, laughing so hard she nearly spilled it. Ned, too, after the first surprise, shook with laughter.

"I know I'm the only man in captivity who ever had to wash his feet before he could go to a fire!"

"MR. NED" AND "MISS ANN," as they called each other, had agreed to provide the music for a Christmas program the next evening at one of the country schools. Miss Ann and her husband came for Ned and Belle in their carriage. Rosa was staying with Will and Rita until they returned, as she did whenever Ned and Belle went out for an evening.

Will and Rita were delighted! They knew as soon as Rosa ate her supper in the kitchen and finished the dishes that Rosa's boy friend, Tom, would tap on the back door. It was Rosa and Tom who had taught the children to play cards. When Tom came in, the four of them sat on the floor in the children's room and played Old Maid and Smut.

It was a clear, cold night for the drive to the country school, but a wrong turn along the way delayed Ned's and Miss Ann's arrival. As soon as they reached the school, Ned and Miss Ann hurried to the stage entrance. When the principal saw them he rushed to the center of the stage and announced to the restless audience, "The music from Dublin have came!"

Ned and Miss Ann could hardly control their laughter, and Ned dared not glance at Belle seated in the audience.

The audience listened to their music with rapt attention and, as always, applauded long and loud. At the end of their final number, two school boys were to draw the curtains from each side. They bowed to the applause and waited—but no curtains.

The principal, by then completely unnerved, loudly whispered, "Curtings!" Nothing happened. Louder he said, "Curtings, please!!" No response.

By this time the audience was beginning to laugh, and Ned and Miss Ann were shaking with mirth though trying to maintain a dignified calm.

Finally, in desperation, the principal shouted, "When I say 'Curtings', give me curtings, *please!!*"

With a quick final bow, Ned and Miss Ann hurried off the stage, without "curtings." Laughing so hard they dared not face the principal, they met Belle and Miss Ann's husband at the carriage and started home. Ned vowed he would never again be able to watch curtains drawn across a stage without laughing.

Miss Ann and her husband left Ned and Belle at their door with gay good nights and much laughter. Belle went on in to see about the children and found them snugly tucked in bed, Rosa sitting in a chair by the fire. Little did she guess that just before she and Ned returned, Tom had disappeared through the back door. Will nor Rita ever mentioned Tom's visits to their parents, for although Rosa said Tom was her brother, they sensed otherwise and seemed to know that Daddy would have put a stop to Tom's visits had he known about them.

IN THE SPRING Rosa finally married Tom and moved to the country to live. No servant ever "quit" the Blackshears; some died, others moved away. Belle had little trouble getting a new cook, for all the Negroes knew that, as in all Southern homes of quality, they would be looked after like a member of the family, though none of them aspired to social equality. Though the pay was small in those days, it cost them little to live. Their house rent was almost nothing and food and clothes presented no problem. Meals were part of the pay, and the cook was also allowed to take "the pan" of leftovers home for her family. Outgrown children's clothes and shoes, men's suits, ladies' dresses and the like were passed along to the servants by those for whom they worked.

Irene, a quiet, efficient servant, took Rosa's place in Belle's kitchen. Irene had several children, but no husband—a not unusual circumstance. She was a good servant and a good mother, and took good care of her children.

But Belle and Ned soon discovered that on Saturday nights Irene's personality was subject to change. It seemed that Saturday was "her night to howl" at the dance halls out in the Negro quarter.

One Monday morning, not long after Irene had come to work for Belle and Ned, she announced at breakfast that she had to "git off an' go to co't."

Ned, rather surprised, asked, "What do you have to go to court for, Irene? Are you in trouble?"

"Yassuh," she replied, "we wuz havin' a dance Saddidy night an' de police arrested me. I tole 'em I cooked fo' Miz Blackshear an' dey let me out to come to work, but said I had to come up befo' de judge dis mawnin' an' pay my fine."

"Surely they don't arrest you for just having a dance, Irene," said Belle.

Sheepishly, Irene said, "No'm. Me an' Viola wuz fightin'."

"What about?" asked Ned.

Irene drew herself up, folded her hands across her ample middle and replied, "I wuz two-steppin' wid a genneman an' Viola she butt up agin me an' we faought!"

Ned and Belle both tried to hide their amusement at this candid admission of guilt.

Ned cleared his throat and said briskly, "Well, you go on with your work, Irene. I'll go up to the courthouse, plead you guilty and take care of it this time. But you behave yourself after this."

"Yassuh, Mr. Blackshear. Thank yo', suh. I sho' ain' gwine do it agin'," she promised as she turned to go into the kitchen.

Irene's promise, however, was short-lived, though often repeated. There were many Monday mornings that Ned appeared in court for her, paid her small fine and returned home to lecture her once more on her Saturday-night behavior. But Irene's virtues as a servant far outweighed these occasional misdemeanors, and the months passed harmoniously in the Blackshear household.

One Monday late in summer, however, Ned came home from court and strode indignantly to the kitchen. That morning the charge against Irene had been more serious—disorderly conduct—and the fine was ten dollars.

As he walked into the kitchen, Ned said sternly, "Irene, I'm getting mighty tired of these fines for your Saturday night misbehavior! This morning I was thoroughly ashamed of my cook being charged with such disgraceful conduct with a man down by the railroad track. The judge fined you ten dollars!"

Irene's eyes and mouth flew open. "I swear 'fo' Gawd, Mr. Blackshear, 'twon't worth it!"

Irene was so surprised—and so sincere—that Ned roared with laughter. Thus ended the lecture, and his good humor was restored.

THE METHODIST CONFERENCE met in Dublin the next fall and Ned and Belle entertained four delegates in their home, two ministers and two laymen. Though Belle was born and reared an Episcopalian, Ned sang in the Methodist church choir and many of their closest friends were Methodists. The cordial hospitality of their home was open to all who came. One of the laymen was V. L. Stanton, brother of Frank L. Stanton, the poet. He was entranced with Ned and Belle and remained a lifelong friend.

Even the children enjoyed the guests who made a jovial group, and the evenings, after the serious business of the day, were filled with laughter and music. To the utter delight and amazement of Will and Rita one of the ministers, Dr. Ryder, could and did stand on his head—a feat unheard of to them for an adult, especially a preacher!

On the last evening of the delegates' visit, after the children had been sent to bed, there was quite a discussion on an erroneous statement made by one of the Dublin laymen at the business session of the conference that morning.

Ned told his guests, "Don't pay any attention to old Harry. Why, I'd bet he doesn't even know who killed cock-robin!"

Dr. Ryder, his eyes twinkling, accepted the challenge. "Who did kill cock-robin?" he asked.

Not one of them knew, and all serious discussion was forgotten in the gales of laughter that followed each person's guess. Ned himself didn't know, though he had brought the subject up.

Finally, his curiosity was not to be denied. He went into Rita's room, waked her and asked if she knew who killed cock-robin.

Sleepily, Rita mumbled, "I, said the sparrow, with my bow and arrow."

The church was filled next morning almost to capacity, as everyone wanted to be there to bid farewell to the visiting ministers and laymen, and to enjoy the program that had been prepared for them. Ned on the violin and Miss Ann at the organ had prepared special music for the occasion.

About midway through the first number, an usher led a late-comer down to one of the few vacant pews at the front. Ned stole a glance in that direction and saw a man with his obviously pregnant wife, followed by their six children. Keeping a straight face, but with a twinkle in his eye, Ned leaned toward Miss Ann and whispered, "Six rattles and a button!"

. Miss Ann had to bow her head to hide her laughter.

As the little Episcopal mission church was not having services this Sunday, Belle and the children had gone with Ned to the Methodist church. After church they were having dinner with Miss Ann and her family, so Belle had told Irene she could have the day off after she baked a ham for their supper.

The Blackshears returned home late that afternoon and found Irene sitting on the back steps, almost panting for breath.

Alarmed, Belle asked, "Irene, what on earth is the matter? Has something happened?"

Wringing her hands, Irene cried, "Oh Lawd, Miss Belle, when I opened my pan at home to give de chillun dey dinner, dere won't nuthin' in dat pan 'cep'n yo' ham! I done got de pans mixed up an' tuck my white folks ham to my house! I run all de way back up here fo' you thought I done stole yo' ham!"

Belle smiled and said reassuringly, "Why, Irene, I know you wouldn't steal my ham."

She opened the door and Irene walked into the kitchen to return the ham and get the other pan. As she walked she muttered to herself, "I never been so 'put out' an' so skeered in my life."

The pans exchanged, Irene went happily on her way to feed her brood.

Ned was in a pensive mood that evening, and after Belle and the children had retired he sat alone on the front veranda. Soon Belle, who was not yet asleep, heard the low sweet strains of Ned's violin. Such exquisite music she had never heard! It was achingly beautiful, part gay, part sad, and Belle listened enthralled. For more than an hour the music went on, and shortly after Ned came in to get ready for bed.

"Are you asleep, Belle?" he whispered.

"No, Mr. Blackshear. I was listening to your music. It was the most beautiful piece I ever heard. What was it?"

"Oh, that wasn't any piece, Belle," he replied, "I was just playing my thoughts."

No doubt wonderful compositions were lost to the world from his inability to read or write music!

When he attended a concert with artists performing, tears of appreciation for the music and the musicians would fill his eyes. When amateurs performed and a discordant note was struck, he winced with real pain. For ragtime he had no use; he called it "musical sacrilege." What a truly great musician he might have been had not the "peddler-professor" given up so easily.

NED HAD NEVER JOINED a church though he was a regular and active attendant. Belle was a dyed-in-the-wool Episcopalian. When Will and Rita reached the age of confirmation, Belle drilled them night after night on the Catechism, preparing them for the Bishop's approaching confirmation visit.

On the Saturday night before Confirmation Sunday, Ned said, "Belle, I've about learned that Catechism you've been teaching the children, so I'm going to be confirmed with them. Grandma Pittman 'Presbyterian baptized' me when I was a baby."

Belle was taken completely by surprise. "Why, Mr. Blackshear! You know you're Methodist in your heart. Why don't you join the Methodist church?"

"Belle, I've been thinking this thing over a long time, and I've come to the conclusion that I'm a little afraid you might get to Heaven and I wouldn't. So, I'm going to join *your* church!"

Thus Ned became an Episcopalian, though he continued to sing in the Methodist choir the Sundays they held no services at the Episcopal mission church.

Many friends came in that evening to congratulate Ned on "finally joining the church." It had been a big day for the whole family and it seemed to Belle that the guests, welcome though they were, would never leave. Yet she hesitated to speed their departure by serving refreshments too soon. As inconspicuously as possible, she managed to get near enough to whisper to Ned, "Mr. Blackshear, what time it it?"

Belle, amused and slightly embarrassed, realized immediately that her whisper was in vain.

Ned announced in his booming voice, "I don't know what time it is, but it's *time!*"

Thus these happy years went on, one by one. The children were fast growing up; Ned's insurance business provided the family's needs and a few luxuries.

Because Ned and Belle were so rich in everything except money, finances were never discussed as being a thing of great importance, especially before the children who were now growing up. More stress was laid on honesty, truthfulness, trustworthiness, loyalty, character and reputation.

The children were never told, "We can't afford for you to do this or go there." Belle would suggest and plan some simpler pleasure. "We'll get a new record and ask some of the girls and boys in to dance. I'll make cookies and hot chocolate."

Her plans were so nice the children were always glad to fall in with them. What fun they had with their little table-model victrola! It had to be cranked and changed after every record, but nobody thought that was a hardship! They took it to picnics and cane grindings and danced on the grass in the moonlight. They went in wagons to these gala occasions, sitting on the pile of soft hay-straw, packed in like sardines; and what a thrill when the boy best liked sat beside the girl he also liked best! How the group sang on the way to and from these parties!

Ned enjoyed his children throughout the years, but now they were teenagers and gave him many anxious and perplexing moments. The home was always full of boys and girls, else his two were going out somewhere. Many evenings "their crowd" met at different homes, played games, danced, and gathered around the piano singing together the popular songs of the day. The one ironclad rule with all the parents was that their girls must be home and say goodnight to their "dates" by eleven o'clock. For a formal dance or special party they were allowed to stay out later, and Ned thought these "special occasions" came around too often.

No "nice" girl ever rode in a buggy or automobile with a

man after dark, nor was she allowed to have more than two dates
a week with the same boy, though she may go with a different
boy every night. The custom of teenagers "going steady" had
not come into vogue.

Every girl had a date on Sunday night and the boys who
couldn't get dates ganged together and went calling en masse
on all the girls and boys who were dating.

How wonderful the stag line was at dances. Girls and their
escorts danced the first and last dances together, but on all the
other dances there were "breaks" every few steps. A girl's popularity was often judged on the number of "breaks" she had.

Ned was particular with his "womenfolks"—not only Rita
but also her cousins and friends who came to visit as house
guests. He thought no man quite worthy of them. The girls
wouldn't have much fun if Belle had not come to the rescue.
She helped them out by making the boys feel welcome. Ned
knew every family in Laurens County, and when the boys came
to call he would invariably say, "Now who was your grandfather?"

Rita would almost cringe when he asked that question, for
she knew full well he was going to spot a "rotten apple" on that
family tree.

"Mother, can't you make Daddy quit asking that question?"
Rita pleaded.

"I wouldn't worry about it, Rita," Belle consoled her. "The
boys don't catch on—they seem flattered by his interest."

After the eleven o'clock "curfew," the girls always went in
to say good night to Rita's parents. That was when Ned would
explode with all the "rotten-apple" reasons why they should
not go with this or that boy. As the girls started to their room,
he would invariably remark, more to himself than to anyone
else, "It's appalling how the bottom rail is getting on top in
society."

One such night he asked Rita's cousin Miriam, "Who came
to see you tonight ?"

"John Sanders, Uncle Ned," she answered.

"Old Long John!" exclaimed Ned. "I'll swear his father

. . ." a long pause while he tried to think of something bad
about John's father—finally, "well, his father had the damned-
est longest arms of any man I ever saw!"

Belle, Miriam and Rita burst into laughter.

Ned went on. "You needn't laugh, for I'll swear he could
stand flat-footed and scratch below his knee."

Their laughter finally shamed him into confessing that he
knew nothing worse on John's father, and his own sense of humor soon had him laughing too.

Ned didn't really think badly of the boys; he was simply
jealous of the evenings "his girls" spent with them when he
could have been enjoying their companionship.

This visit of Miriam's was during a depression year, when
there were many "successful" fires in small businesses. There
was scarcely a night when the alarm didn't sound. Miriam and
Rita did not tell Belle and Ned, but each night when the boys
were leaving they would whisper, "Will I see you at the fire?"

"Yes!"

Their parents never caught on to why the girls and boys
were so "primped up" in the middle of the night to go to see
the "fire!"

DURING THIS TEENAGE ERA, Uncle Caesar, a faithful servant now nearing eighty years old, came every afternoon to cut splinters to keep the wood boxes full. He spoke bluntly and in a gruff-sounding voice. In winter he came early every morning to make the fires.

As soon as the fire in his bedroom was made, Ned would get up in his long white split-up-the-side nightshirt, put his hat on to keep the fire glare out of his sensitive eyes, and take a seat in the big rocking chair before the fire. On very cold mornings, he would tell Uncle Caesar to sit on the wood box and get warm.

Belle was amused at the conversations between them. Talking more to himself than to the old darkie, Ned said, "I don't like my daughter going out with all these boys. They are forever under foot in this house. First thing we know she'll fancy herself in love with some young whippersnapper she knows nothing about and want to marry him."

"Well, Marse Ned," consoled Uncle Caesar, "she ain' never gwine know a man nohow 'til she winters wid 'im."

"Maybe so, maybe so," agreed Ned, "but these young folks are going at a mighty fast trot—a dance here and a party there, something every night."

Uncle Caesar punched the fire with the poker, and in his deliberate manner said, "Well, Marse Ned, when de mammy trots an' de pappy trots you cain't 'spec' de colts to pace."

Belle, who had overheard this early morning philosophy, shook with laughter—remembering only too well Ned's "trotting" in his youthful days.

One morning a few days before Thanksgiving, Belle interrupted their "wood box conversation."

"Uncle Caesar, my cook is sick and I must find someone to dress my turkey. Do you know anyone who will do it for me?"

"Yas'm, Miss, I'll dress it," he said.

Surprised, Belle said, "I didn't know you could dress a turkey, Uncle Caesar."

"Yas'm," he assured her, "or air other insec' you wants to eat."

Somewhat taken aback, Belle said, "Well, I'll let you know if I need you."

Needless to say, that was the last time Belle mentioned the turkey to Uncle Caesar.

One stormy winter morning shortly after Thanksgiving, faithful Uncle Caesar showed up, drenched to the skin. He made the fires and sat on the wood box to thaw and dry out. Ned, nightshirt and hat, had just seated himself.

Belle said, "Uncle Caesar, you should not have come out in this storm."

"Miss, dis ain' no sto'm atall. You orter seed one I wuz in one time! It blowed de trees up by de roots, blowed down de barns, blowed off de housetops, blowed de horses an' cows an' pigs off dey feet—why, it even blowed de guts outen de chickens!"

Belle was horrified at this inelegance of expression, but Ned's laughter rang through the house.

Belle quickly changed the subject. "Mr. Blackshear," she said, "Will is coming home tomorrow for the Christmas holidays, you know, and there's a lot to do. I want you to get some things downtown for me today if this storm lets up."

"Just give me your list, Belle. Is Lewis coming with Will?" he asked.

"Yes, he is," she replied, "it will be good to have the house full of young folks again."

Will and his cousin Lewis had gone away to military school that fall, and Belle could hardly wait to see her beloved son again, though she had tried desperately not to show how much she had missed him. Lewis was spending the holidays with them as his parents had gone away to be with their married daughter who was expecting her first child.

The two boys had grown up together and Lewis was almost like a son to Belle and Ned. He and Will had always shared a mutual love of hunting and fishing. Uncle Caesar's son, Steve, had kept their hunting dogs for them, and Will and Lewis always took Steve on their hunting trips. But Steve would not be there to welcome them home this time—he had been killed in a shooting accident just a month before. Belle had not written this news to Will because she knew how it would grieve him. She thought it would be easier to tell him when he was home where she could comfort him and help to ease the shock.

Belle invited several of the boys and girls for dinner the next night to welcome Will and Lewis home. There was a lot of excitement in the air and much gaiety in the crowd. During dinner Ned remembered about Steve and said, "Will, did you and Lewis know Uncle Caesar's boy Steve was shot and killed here a few weeks ago?"

"No, sir," said Will, "how did it happen, Daddy?"

"I don't really know, Will. Uncle Caesar told us it happened, but you know him—he didn't volunteer any information, and he was so grieved we hated to ask."

Lewis joined in and asked, "Where did he get shot, Cousin Ned? Was he hunting or fighting?"

Just at that moment, Uncle Caesar passed the dining room door with his arms full of wood to replenish the living room fire, and before Ned could answer, Lewis called out, "Uncle Caesar, where did Steve get shot?"

Gruffly Uncle Caesar answered, "Right under de lef' titty!" and kept on walking.

The boys and girls were taken aback at this reply and blushed to the roots of their hair. Belle was embarrassed too. But Ned's eyes were dancing with mirth as Belle made a noble effort to change the topic of conversation—she could always "save the day" in any situation.

WHEN, SEVERAL YEARS LATER, Rita chose to marry Jim Dickens, strangely enough Ned found no objection to this handsome Virginian—perhaps because he was eleven years her senior and was well established in the hardware business in Halifax, Virginia. Uncle Caesar remarked, "Mr. Ned went far beyant my expectancy when he let Miss Rita git married."

Ned told Jim, "I just hate to have her move so far away from home."

Jim consoled him as best he could, and said "She can come back to visit once a year, Mr. Blackshear, and you and Mrs. Blackshear must visit us once a year."

Thus Ned became reconciled.

Rita's first visit home was the following November. Jim joined her for Christmas week to take her back to Virginia in early January. Such wining and dining and partying of every description went on while Jim was there. This was quite different from their quiet life in quaint little Halifax.

Enroute home Jim asked Rita, "Don't those men in Dublin ever work?"

"Sure," she replied, "they work hard all year, but this was Christmas when everyone celebrates."

Rita didn't get home the next Christmas because she was expecting her first baby. Ned and Belle came to Virginia in the fall to be with their daughter through that "blessed event," and she had a precious little girl, their first grandchild. Ned was beside himself with anxiety which was followed by great joy.

They hated to leave the grandchild, but Ned announced one

day at breakfast, " We must go home, Belle. My troublesome teeth have flared up again."

"Dr. Summers told you to have them pulled several months ago," Belle said, scolding him a little.

"Well, I must get back and let Doc get started."

A few days later, Jim and Rita put them on the train for home amid tearful goodbyes.

Belle wrote that Ned had begun his ordeal with the dentist, and sometime later Rita received this letter from Ned:

DEAR DAUGHTER,

I have something on my mind that I want to tell you about. I hope you never have the same experience. I want you to know I have my false teeth and as near as possible want to describe how my mouth felt and still feels with these teeth in.

If they were of a religious sect I'd call them Holy Rollers. They roll over when in service and are a sect unto themselevs. They are opposed to eating, they stopped my whistling, I can't even chew gruel, and they insist that I talk the foreign tongue. The truth is this old man, about the mouth, has been made new and the things he once loved to eat he hates because these teeth refuse to stay put when he puts them.

Why, I can't sneeze, I can't even blow my nose without using both hands and a handkerchief to catch the darn things in the air— they are not actually blown out of my mouth but I'm sure every time they will be.

If I could parse or decline them they could not be parsed as the neuter gender because they are neither inanimate nor inactive. Surely they are not of the possessive case, for I'm never certain they are mine. They must be of the objective case for I have not found anything they are willing to do. If they can be termed of the animal kingdom they are of the bucking Mexican pony variety. They refuse to be ridden by the most delicate food; they lie down, turn over or do anything to spill the rider.

The upper ones are getting broken to the bridle but please don't try to saddle 'em because if you do old Joe begins to kick up from behind and before and the bottom ones kick up behind old Joe.

My dentist told me I must sleep with them—I do, with them on their side of the bed and me on mine.

At first I was sure it was Syracuse, N. Y., I had in my mouth; in

several days I found out that was a mistake, it was only Greensboro,
North Carolina, but I have the assurance that in ten to twelve
months time I will find out it was only Brewton and finally little
Condor, Georgia. But this I do know—there is no room for teeth
and food in my mouth, but I am determined to wear 'em. They can
rear and they can pitch—they can cast me in the ditch—but I will
shut down with my mouth and I will follow, North or South—they
are *my* teeth! I will wear 'em—I shall let nobody share 'em! Whoa,
Betsy! Let me get astride—because I'm "gwine" to ride! I shut
both eyes and swallow by faith—it may be soup, it may be fish—
more often the thing I little wish—whether applesauce or butter—
these my teeth refuse to cut 'er.

They know I'm writing about them; these lower ones have just
raised up on their elbows to listen.

I have written this foolishness to amuse you, not to punish nor
to educate you. When one has swinging teeth like the old oaken
bucket that hangs in the well he forgets all about ideals, and while
he is head and tails in the air trying to adjust to the teeth, he has
only the inclination to pick a good landing place.

YOUR DEVOTED DAD.

The following summer Rita took the baby to Dublin and
showed her off with pride. At the end of the visit Jim came to
take them home. He was entertained every day with picnics,
boat rides, swimming parties, etc. Swimming at Wells' Spring
on the afternoon of his last day there, he walked over to Rita
on the bank of the spring and said, "You know, I never have
seen 'Christmas' last as long in one place as it does in Dublin!"

Two happy years went by and a little boy was born to Rita
and Jim. Jim and Ned were jubilant. Belle and Rita smiled and
winked at each other, for they knew that with all the "carrying
on" the men were doing, there was nothing to equal the pride
and quiet joy in the heart of a mother who has given birth to
a son.

BORN OF NED'S GREAT LOVE for people was the overwhelming kindness of his nature. He owned a little house on the back of his home lot which faced another street. This he rented for a nominal sum and Belle was to have the rent for any little extra extravagance that she wished. All went well until Bob Baker, his wife and their six children moved into the house.

Bob never could quite pay all of the rent and finally, toward the end of the year, he stopped making the effort to pay anything.

"Mr. Blackshear, has Mr. Baker paid his rent this month?" Belle asked.

"Not yet."

"Did he ever catch up on the back rent?"

"No, Belle," he sheepishly replied.

"Mr. Blackshear, you are too kind for your own good. Why don't you get Mr. Baker out of that house and get a good renter?"

"Belle, I realize I have a legal right to put old Baker out, but I seriously doubt if I have a moral right to put a man with a wife and six children out in the cold, knowing he hasn't enough money to rent another house."

So Bob Baker stayed on until he burned all the fence palings, every loose board, and finally the doorsteps, trying to keep his family warm. By spring the house was too dilapidated for use, and Baker moved out of his own accord and went to live with one of his more prosperous relatives. Then Ned had the house repaired and secured a better renter!

While Ned and Belle were discussing Bob Baker and his non-existent rent, Walter, the colored janitor at the nearby Baptist church, walked up to the steps, removed his hat, and said, "Mawnin', Mr. Ned."

"What's on your mind, Walter?" Ned asked.

"It's Ella, sir. I jes' cain' rest for thinkin' 'bout her."

"Is she still in Atlanta?" Ned asked.

"Yassuh. It's been nigh on to a year since she lef', an' now she don' answer my letters. Everybody say she done quit me."

"I'm sorry to hear that, Walter," Ned said consolingly, "but if it's true, why don't you think about getting you another wife? Your preacher's daughter, Sally, thinks a lot of you and she'd make you a good wife."

Few Southern Negroes got divorces—when they "lost dere taste for dat Nigger" they simply married another one. It was an accepted custom.

"Well, Mr. Ned," Walter explained, twisting his old felt hat in his hands, "is you ever been in a shoe sto' with hundreds o' shoe boxes up side both walls? You looks at 'em an' looks at 'em, but out o' all dem shoes dey ain' but one pair in dat sto' you'd have! Well, dat's de way I feels about Ella!"

Ned's sympathetic heart was touched by Walter's story. "God bless you, Walter. We'll see if we can't get Ella back somehow."

Walter smiled for the first time, confident that Mr. Ned would help him, and went back to his janitor duties at the church across the street.

Belle, who had been listening, said, "How kind you are to people in trouble, Mr. Blackshear."

"Well, Belle," Ned said, "when a man—black or white—loves his wife that much, I'd do anything to help bring them together."

"What can you do?" she asked.

"I'm going to write Ella a letter right now and enclose a railroad ticket from Atlanta to Dublin."

He arose and went in to write the letter. No one ever knew what he wrote except he and Ella, but in two weeks she was back home with Walter, where she stayed the rest of her life.

Belle remained seated on the porch absorbed in thoughts of the kindness of this man who was her husband. She smiled to herself as she thought of his most ridiculous kind act, of the night he was awakened from a sound sleep by hearing a man snoring outside the window. He had pulled his trousers on over his nightshirt and gone out to look for the source of the snoring. Under the edge of the house was a man, deep in alcoholic slumber. Ned roused him, supported him into the house, got him into the tub for a bath, then had put him to bed in the guest room. Belle had long ago become resigned to the fact that "Mr. Blackshear is unpredictable," so Ned's putting this strange drunk man to bed in her guest room did not upset her.

CHAPTER

# XXIV

NED WAS A TEMPERATE DRINKER, and only occasionally had an old fashioned toddy in the late afternoon. The only time he ever drank too much was the night in 1892 when Grover Cleveland was re-elected President. Most Southern Democrats went on a wild celebration that night.

Telling Rita about it in later years, he said, "I arrived home in the wee small hours feeling sick as a dog with nausea. Belle wouldn't get the slop-jar, she wouldn't hold my head, she wouldn't bathe my face. After surviving that night I never got drunk again."

He was not so temperate in eating! He enjoyed good food, ate heartily three times a day and never had indigestion. In fact, his health was perfect, but his imagination so magnified any minor ailment that the grunting and groaning would often cause the family to remark, "Listen to Daddy enjoying his poor health."

If he read a medicine ad he would swear he had every described symptom that the ad claimed to cure. The family would have to laugh him out of it or he would surely buy the "cure." If he was, as on a few occasions, given a prescription, he always took double what the directions said—his theory being "if a teaspoonful will help me, two teaspoons full will do me twice as much good." He doubled up on a laxative dose one night and that cured him of this habit!

Ned's close friends knew how his imagination worked—in fact, Ned had laughed with them about it many times. One day some of the men whose offices were in the same building as his decided to play what they thought would be a practical joke on Ned.

Dr. Summers, whose dental offices were just across the hall, came into Ned's office where Ned was going over some insurance policies. Ned looked up as he entered, "Morning, Doc, how goes it with you?"

"Fine, Ned fine," he replied, "how're you today?"

"Oh, fit as a fiddle I guess." Ned noticed a surprised look on Doc's face. "What's the matter, Doc, did I say something wrong?"

"No, not a thing, Ned," he said, "I'm just glad to hear you feel good, as I thought you looked a little pale. Glad you're okay—see you later."

Ned had hardly gotten back to his work when Mr. Llewelyn came in from his office next door.

"Come in, Lew, come in," greeted Ned. Then, noticing Lew's expression, he asked, "What's the matter with you?"

"Why, nothing, Ned—I'm fine," he said, "but you don't look so good—kinda pale around the gills today. Don't you feel good?" A look of real concern showed on his face.

Ned, with a little sigh, said, "Well, I don't feel quite up to par this morning."

"You take care of yourself, old man. See you later." Lew hurried out to hide a smile at how the joke was going.

In about thirty minutes, Colonel Wade, a lawyer with offices down the hall, came in to see Ned on the pretext of business. Ned, in a slightly subdued voice, said, "Come in, Wade, have a seat. What can I do for you?"

Colonel Wade started to sit down, then changed his mind saying, "I came in to talk about some insurance, Ned, but I can see you're a sick man. We'll talk another day."

Ned, nodding his head just slightly, said, "If it isn't urgent, Colonel, I'd just as soon put if off. I do feel terrible this morning!"

As Colonel Wade left, Ned put his elbows on the desk and rested his head in his hands as he pondered over what could have made him so sick today!

He was still sitting thus when Mr. Hammond came in from his real estate office at the end of the hall. Ned didn't even look up until Mr. Hammond touched him on the shoulder. As he looked up weakly, with his eyes half-closed, Hammond exclaimed, "My God, Ned, you're a sick man! Is there anything I can do for you?"

Ned, his voice weak and trembling, said, "Call me a hack, Hammond. I've got to go home and I'm too sick to walk. Then find Dr. Biggs and tell him to come to my house as quick as he can."

Ned went home in the hack and, to Belle's dismay, took to his bed with much moaning and groaning.

Hammond called Dr. Biggs, told him the joke they had played on Ned, and said, "I'm afraid we have really made him sick, Doc, so please go see about him."

Dr. Biggs found Ned groaning and tossing upon his bed. He told Belle that Ned's friends had conspired to play a joke on him to see if they could make him think he was sick and the joke had gone beyond their expectations. "I've prescribed a few harmless sugar pills that the drug store will send you, and told Ned he'll be all right before morning."

Dr. Biggs then went directly to Ned's office building, called all the culprits into Wade's office and read them "the riot act" about playing such a dastardly trick on a man with Ned's imagination.

The next day they all apologized to Ned when he came to work, and he had a good laugh with them about it.

"By the way, Belle told me to tell you all she is expecting you tonight. It's her turn to have our supper and we'll have a good game afterwards."

Each week these friends met at different homes for a friendly game of poker. Once a month each wife would be hostess and provide a good supper for the men. "Chit'lins" were their favorite dish, but were not always available.

"Belle couldn't get 'chit'lins', but she'll fix us up a good supper anyway."

"Tell Miss Belle we'll be there," said Colonel Wade, "no man in his right mind would miss one of her suppers."

As they walked into the dining room that night their eyes lit up with pleasant anticipation as they viewed the huge platter piled high with pigs feet which had been dipped in batter and fried to a golden brown. There was a big bowl of grits, turnip greens and baked sweet potatoes. There were hot biscuits and cornbread; that was a meal to these men's liking. Ben, who was always hired to help out on these evenings, served it to perfection.

There were no ladies present except the hostess. The men were bountifully served and eating heartily when suddenly Ned said, "Excuse me," and left the table hurriedly.

This was a most unusual occurence. Belle was alarmed and perplexed, but tried not to show it before her guests. Ned stayed so long that finally she could stand it no longer.

"If you gentlemen will excuse me I'll see what is the matter with Mr. Blackshear."

She went in search of him and found him on the bed, violently nauseated, his head hanging over the slop-jar. Alarmed, Belle asked, "Why, Mr. Blackshear, what is the matter with you?"

"Belle," he moaned, "one of those chickens Irene cooked was deformed. I ate some of it before I got that peculiar little bone in my mouth."

When she could stop laughing Belle said, "You weren't eating chicken, Mr. Blackshear; those are pigs feet."

He bounced off the bed. "Pigs feet! Why in the devil didn't you tell me they were pigs feet!"

He strode back to the dining room, helped himself to more pigs feet and was, as usual, the life of the party.

Ben helped Irene remove the dishes and while she cleaned up the kitchen he busied himself getting the table and everything ready for the poker game.

Ben was "Brother Jackson" to the colored congregation he preached to on Sundays. During the week he worked different days as "yard man" for several families. He liked to "help out" nights when his white folks gave parties because there were big tips in it for him. He was very proficient in the art of serving, and was typical of what Southerners call "a white folks' Nigger."

As he was getting out the cards and poker chips Ned said, "Ben, where did you get that little white horse dangling from your watch fob?"

"I served a party for Mr. and Mrs. Adams las' night, Mr. Ned, and Mr. Adams give it to me 'cause I thought it was purty."

"Ben, you know that came off a Scotch whisky bottle. What will your congregation say about that when you preach to them tomorrow?"

"Dem fo'ks I preach to ain' gwine know where it come from 'cause dey ain' never seed no Scotch whisky." Ben joined in with the men's laughter.

Ned's Negro friends afforded him many laughs but he never ridiculed them. They were his friends whom he liked and respected.

The game over, Ned saw his friends to the door. Belle had retired to her room immediately after supper because the men liked these poker evenings to be strictly a stag affair.

"Hurry and clean up this mess, Ben, so you can go home and I can lock the doors and get some sleep."

"While I do dis, Mr. Ned, I wonder if you could he'p me out wid sumpin' about one o' my church members?" Ben asked.

"What's the trouble, Ben?"

"Could you he'p me git the doctor to do sumpin' about Dinah Jones' daughter Sary?"

"Maybe," said Ned, "what is the matter with Dinah's daughter? Is she sick?"

Ben was gathering up cards and chips while he talked. His head cocked a little to one side, "She ain' zackly sick, Mr. Ned."

"Well, what exactly is it?" prompted Ned.

Ben stopped putting the chips in the box as he got more serious. "Sary she done got three chillun wid no pa and now she gwine have 'nother one, and she leaves 'em home wid Dinah to tend to while she off workin' an' gallivantin'."

Ned, smiling to himself, said, "What do you and Dinah think the doctor could do about that?"

"Well," said Ben, thoughtfully scratching his head, "Dinah an' me thought maybe he could do sumpin' to cut her nature down."

Ned could not restrain his roaring laughter. Ben laughed, too, though he had no idea what was so funny.

"Ben, I'm afraid the doctor couldn't do much about that. You're her preacher—you'll just have to talk to Sary about her sins and pray for her. Try to get her to marry herself a good husband that'll look after her and the kids and make her behave herself."

"Yassuh, Mr. Ned," said Ben, "I sho' will. Dat gal is sho' a worry to her ma."

Ben finished straightening up the room and said good night. Ned locked the back door after him, then went quietly into his room so as not to wake Belle.

BELLE WAS ALWAYS BUSY, not only at home but in civic and charity work. Through the years she held many responsible positions, among them president of Oconee Chapter, U. D. C., historian for John Laurens Chapter, D.A.R., was prominent in Red Cross work, and president of the Associated Charities in Laurens County.

While serving in the latter capacity, there was a colored woman who came every year asking for funds to finance the coming new baby. The third time, Belle said, "Rachel, why don't you stop having a baby every year? You know you can't afford it!"

"Yas'm, I knows it," she replied, "but I jes' hates to deny my ole man his only pleasure."

Ned wasn't much of a joiner of clubs but was very civic-minded and intensely interested in all political affairs, county, state and national. During any major campaign he read every word printed in the *Macon Telegraph, Atlanta Journal* and *Atlanta Constitution,* pro and con about each candidate. He never failed to vote and always for the man he believed best fitted for the office—provided, of course he was a Democrat!

Ned could not accept any evil nor did he try to come to the best possible terms with the conventional evils of seeing our country dominated by power politicians, greed and lawlessness. He made no compromise with TRUTH. He felt it his Christian duty to speak against wrong with his voice and his pen. If his opinion was proven wrong he had the courage to reverse himself. He voted against women's suffrage, and wrote articles against it for the hometown paper. His main objection was that voting cheapened womanhood and that it was beneath the dignity of a real lady to be seen at political polls. He could never lower his high standard and respect for womanhood. He put them on a pedestal and they remained there throughout his life.

During World War I, Ned became interested in and campaigned for national prohibition. He was sincere in his belief that whisky could and should be outlawed, and cast his vote accordingly.

During the ensuing years, however, Ned came to realize that the 18th Amendment was a farce. He saw men and women, who never before had been intemperate, take to drinking any bootleg alcoholic beverage obtainable. "Moonshine" and "home brew," even raw alcohol, were being sold and served, at premium prices —the criminals were creating bootleg empires that seemed almost beyond reach of the law. Ned grieved over the death and destruction, blindness and moral laxity that seemed to descend upon the nation like a plague. It broke his heart to see so many fine young men—his own son among them—become almost hopeless alcoholics.

Stronger than he had fought for prohibition, Ned worked for its repeal. He wrote letters to friends and relatives throughout the South, and wrote article after article for the newspapers.

A delegation of Dublin ministers, shocked that a man of his high caliber would favor repeal, called on him one day to try to discourage his campaign. They debated the question all afternoon, and so convincing were Ned's arguments, the entire delegation based their sermons the following Sunday on Ned's suggested theme, "Morals cannot be legislated into people."

After a card game one night, Belle and Ned sat talking, hopingWill would come home soon.

"Mr. Blackshear, do you suppose Will will ever settle down and get married?"

"I'm afraid not, Belle," he answered, with a sigh, "he is quite a 'ladies' man,' but he considers his love affairs lightly."

"Have you noticed how often he stops by next door and talks to little Sue McKendree?"

"That has me worried, too," said Ned. "Will is a fascinating man and Sue is too young and unwise in the ways of the world to be exposed to a man like Will."

"It would be a regrettable thing if she falls in love with him and gets hurt by his insincerity."

Though Belle loved her son deeply, she was well aware of his inner weakness.

"I'm going over there tomorrow," Ned decided, "and tell Sue's mother to stop Will's visits because I fear his intentions are not honorable."

"I think you should," agreed Belle, "it might forestall a heartbreak."

"Well, we might as well go to bed now, Belle. Will may not come in at all tonight."

But Will had at last lost his heart and fallen deeply in love with Sue. Her black eyes, jet black hair, her lovely smile and her innocence had ensnared him.

He brought her home one night soon after, and announced that they had just been married at the minister's home. Sue was a delightful addition to the family and fit into their home and hearts immediately. She loved Will devotedly, and no man ever had a better wife. For a few years Will moderated his drinking and was true to his marriage vows, but, alas! he had not the strength of character nor self-mastery to remain firm—whisky and women got their hold on him again.

After eleven short, happy years, Rita was left a widow by Jim's untimely death. With her two children she returned to Dublin to live with Ned and Belle. Will and Sue were living at home, too. A young, efficient colored girl, Mary Lou, was now cooking for the family.

The most notable changes in the eleven years Rita had lived in Virginia were that Will had become an alcoholic and Ned's fingers were so stiffened with rheumatism that he could no longer play his beloved violin. And, like his father before him, Ned's eyesight was very poor. One eye had been successfully operated on for a cataract, but he had no sight in the other eye. He could

no longer see well enough to operate his insurance agency, so it
was sold.

These afflictions neither saddened nor embittered Ned. He
was still his gay, lovable and entertaining self. He could still
manage to read his newspapers and, by the "hunt and peck" system on his portable typewriter, he could write letters and articles
for the paper. He enjoyed his friends who came often to visit or
to play Setback. The card table was never folded and put away
because it was daily in use. Belle played if they needed a fourth;
if not, she sat near by and read or crocheted.

One winter Sue was ill with flu, and across the hall in another
room Will was on a "spree." Old Bob, one of the Blackshear
Negroes from the country, stayed in town overnight to "wait
on Mr. Will." The doctor had prescribed fresh orange juice for
Sue. The oranges were placed on a table in the hall for easy
access when Sue needed them. Sue, sick and worried about Will,
could not sleep. Will, nervous from drink, stayed awake all night.
Every time the old Negro would doze, Sue would hear Will say,
"Bob, Oh, Bob, let's eat a orange!"

By daylight, these two had consumed all of Sue's oranges!

Lest Bob should doze again, Will said, "Bob, go in the bathroom and bring my toothbrush, a glass of water and the tooth
paste."

Bob returned with the water and brush, and said, "Mr. Will,
I ain't never seed no tooth paste. What do it look like?"

"It's a tube, three or four inches long."

"Yessir."

Bob went back to look for it. In a few minutes he came back
to the room, beaming. "Here 'tis, Mr. Will," he said, and handed
him the roll of toilet paper!

Only when Will was drinking would he be unfaithful to
Sue. There was a woman who lived in a neighboring town—
we'll call it Jenkinsville—and he would go there and pick up
this woman and off they would go. Three or four days later, he
would come home—sick, broke and very remorseful.

One day, when he had just started drinking, he was standing on a corner in Dublin waiting for traffic to pass so he could cross the street. A tourist slowed his car and called, "Friend, can you tell me how long it will take me to get to Jenkinsville?"

"Yes, sir," Will replied. "You really asked the right man! It will take you forty-five minutes to get there and three days to get back!"

For thirteen years, Will's behavior went from bad to worse, and became so unbearable and embarrassing that Belle and Ned advised Sue to go to her brother's home in another town in the hope that this would bring Will to his senses. She left in tears, saying, "I'll be back when Will comes for me sober."

Will loved Sue and was miserable without her. He went many times to get Sue, starting out sober and hopeful, but would be drunk before he arrived. She came back twice, but poor Will was too weak to mend his ways, and heartbroken Sue would return to her brother's home. Will's family grieved deeply over this situation and did all that was possible to remedy it, but to no avail. So, invoking the family philosophy of "If there's a remedy try to find it; if there's none never mind it," life went on in the home much as it had before.

IN NED'S EIGHTIETH YEAR he had his first serious illness. Not even the doctors thought he would recover, but they reckoned without his wonderful constitution! What Belle and Rita would have done without faithful Mary Lou to help through his illness is problematical.

It was a happy day when he had convalesced sufficiently to have his meals in the dining room once more! Mary Lou served his soup and hoe-cake cornbread—Ned never could stand crackers with soup! He was so audibly enjoying his food that Belle said, "Mr. Blackshear, I hear you like the soup."

Ned looked up and said, "Belle, don't try to teach me any table manners today. You know when you take the s-s-s-o-o-oop out of soup it's not worth a damn!"

Ned continued to improve, and with the advent of spring he spent many hours sitting in the warm sun on the side porch—sometimes reading, sometimes writing, often "just thinking." On the afternoon of his birthday, Belle joined him on the porch and found him "pecking" out a letter on his typewriter.

"What are you writing, Mr. Blackshear?" she asked him.

"A few birthday thoughts, Belle, to Miss Jennie and Miss Virgie," he said. Miss Jennie and Miss Virgie were old-maid sisters, friends of Ned in his young manhood.

Belle sat down in a rocking chair and said, "How about reading it to me."

Ned smiled and took the paper out of the typewriter as he said, "All right—but it's just a bit of foolishness."

Belle listened appreciatively as he read.

Three score and twelve and then an eight
And you will have my years.
They're filled with sunny memories
Mingled with burning tears.

This life we live in this old world
Is never free from sin.
When Adam ate forbidden fruit
The Devil entered in.

We have been hungry since that day
For that same kind of fruit.
We may have other kinds galore
But only apples suit.

And they from that forbidden tree
Are still considered best.
That Eve knew this is reason why
She passed by all the rest.

Jealous of Adam's appetite,
Eve ate one from this tree,
Then said to Adam, "Have a bite,
The best I give to thee."

He looked into her loving eyes,
Forgot forbidden tree—
Forgot the fruit which grew thereon,
But not "the best for thee."

These her words rang in his ears;
She must surely love me!
And true love casteth out all fears,
Was his soliloquy.

'Twas then first time he saw her dress—
Fig leaves pinned together
He thought the dress was rather scant
But it was springtime weather.

She had no needle, cloth or thread
But, true to womanhood,
She found these small fig leaves instead
And made small pins of wood.

He saw the love light in her eyes
And all else was forgot.
That light was love, and love said eat
If it be right or not.

And love still has the right of way
O, let that love be pure!
If consecrated, it will save;
If not, will damn you sure.

God bless you both and the memories which come to me as I think of you. There are some shadows, but all pictures of the "beautiful" must go through darkrooms in development, and have a dark background. Goodness and sadness make up life; tears beautify and bless—but, oh, the sunshine follows, and there is light and love.

NED BLACKSHEAR.

When he finished reading, Belle said, "Why that wasn't foolishness, Mr. Blackshear. It was lovely. I declare, you constantly amaze me with your writings even after all these years."

Just then Mary Lou came out to tell them dinner was ready. Ned's appetite had gotten back to normal and he looked forward to mealtime three times a day. Much to Ned's delight, the dessert turned out to be his favorite—blackberry dumpling with hard sauce.

"I swear this is good, Belle," he remarked. "I believe I could eat my old shoe soles if you put hard sauce on 'em." He picked up his empty dish. "Could I have a little more?"

"Mr. Blackshear, I don't think you should," Belle said. "It's so rich, I'm afraid it might make you sick again."

Ned turned to Rita. "Daughter, your mother won't even give me enough to eat," he complained.

"Mother," Rita said, "Daddy is eighty years old and has always eaten whatever he wanted. Why not give it to him."

At that, Ned said, "Belle, I do believe Rita's trying to kill me!"

Belle and Rita burst out laughing at Ned's problem—to be starved to death or fed to death. He solved it by having more dessert, but only half as much as he wanted.

After dinner Belle and Rita sat on the porch talking.

"Mother," Rita asked, "why do you suppose old men eat so much?"

"I don't know, Rita," she replied, "unless it's the only appetite they have left that they can satisfy!"

Rita was shocked speechless—that was the first inelegant thing she'd ever heard her mother say. Though Belle had borne four children, Rita had often wondered if she really knew "the facts of life"—she surely had never told them to her! And Rita could well remember when she and Will were children that Belle would wash their mouths with soap if they used any word that Belle thought the least bit "off color" or inelegant.

After supper, Belle went into the living room where Ned sat reading his paper. She picked up her sewing basket and sat down just as Mary Lou came to the living room door.

"What is it, Mary Lou?" Belle asked. "Come on in."

Mary Lou came just inside the door—dressed in the whitest white party dress Belle had ever seen, white stockings, white shoes and even a wide white ribbon on her kinky, black hair. Belle tried to hide her smile as Mary Lou said, "Mrs. Blackshear, kin I go look at myse'f in the long hat-rack mirror? I don' wanna be late, so I changed my clothes in the kitchen."

As Mary Lou preened herself before the mirror of the hat-rack, Ned looked up from his reading and stared. "My God, Mary Lou," he said, "you look like a fly in a pitcher of buttermilk!"

At that Belle laughed, as did Mary Lou. Ned went back to his paper and Belle to her crocheting. They both thought Mary Lou must have gone and were startled when, thirty minutes later, she again appeared at the door.

"Is anything wrong, Mary Lou?" asked Belle.

"Naw'm," she said, "I jest thought I'd let you know I wuz goin', Mrs. Blackshear."

"Where are you going so dressed up, Mary Lou," Ned asked, "to a party?"

"Not zackly, Mr. Blackshear," she said "I'se gittin' married agin tonight."

Ned put down his paper. "I thought you had a husband, Mary Lou," he said. "What happened to Sam?"

"We quit, Mr. Blackshear. Sam won't a bit o' good. Besides, I done los' my taste for dat Nigger," she explained.

Ned spoke sternly to her and said, "You ought to be ashamed of yourself, Mary Lou—marrying and quitting, quitting and marrying every few months or so. Don't you know that's a sin? You are living in adultery. You'll never get to Heaven, Mary Lou, unless you mend your ways—Hell will get you sure."

Mary Lou had listened respectfully and when Ned stopped she said, in all seriousness, "I don' know so much 'bout if I'se goin' to Hebbin or Hell, Mr. Blackshear, but I sho' is crazy 'bout dat thing you calls 'dult'ry!" Turning to leave the room, she said, "Good night, Mrs. Blackshear."

"Good night, Mary Lou," Belle said, trying hard to hide her amusement.

Ned "just sat," looking a bit stunned, and feeling a bit foolish.

Belle laughed as she said, "Mr. Blackshear, that is the first time I've ever seen you left without a comeback speech in your efforts to reform a sinner."

"Humpph!" he said, finally, trying to ignore Belle's laughter, and went back to reading his paper.

# XXVII

WHEN NED WAS EIGHTY-THREE, his beloved Cousin Annie passed away in Marianna. This was a shock and deep grief to him. After her death the old White home came into his possession. He and Belle decided to go back to Marianna to live their remaining years in the home where Ned had spent so many happy years with Auntie and Annie and where together he and Belle had spent the first year of their married life. So the family—Ned, Belle, Will, Rita and her children—moved to Marianna.

With the home they also "inherited" old Mollie who had "waited on Miss Annie" for thirty years. Mollie was seventy-five years old. She was a splendid cook but her mind was a bit "off" on the subject of religion. The contours of her face and the expression of her eyes were ape-like, but she was a dear, good soul. She wore a man's old felt hat, brim turned down all around, and it was next to impossible to get her to remove it.

Belle preferred a younger servant, so she hired one and told Mollie she could not use her. This did not faze Mollie; she came to work every morning. Her only explanation was "I'se gwine stay on here 'cause I wuz Miss Annie's right han' an' I'se sho' gwine look after her house an' her fo'ks."

Every day she told Belle, "You is purty as an angel an' sweet as Hebbin." Could be that consoled Belle for having to keep Mollie on! And the family grew fond of Mollie—as of all who had served them so faithfully throughout the years—she was so good and so kind.

One night Rita gave a dinner party for some of her new Marianna friends. After everything had been prepared, all Mollie

had to do was cook and serve hot biscuits. That afternoon Rita
said, "Mollie, please don't wear that old hat tonight."

"All right, ma'am" agreed Mollie without hesitation.

Rita thought a victory had really been won.

The guests were seated and their plates served when Mollie
walked in to pass hot biscuits. She had on her "best dress" and
on her head perched a tiny round black hat with a six-inch green
ostrich plume sticking straight up from the back which waved
and bobbed with each step she took around the table.

Rita was first startled, then embarrassed, and finally hilarious
as the whole party joined in laughter at old Mollie's efforts to
dress up for "Miss Rita's party."

Monday morning after the party the family was discussing
at breakfast a movie they had seen the night before. Belle interrupted them and said, "Don't mention movie when Mollie is in
the room, please. You know how she can rant and rave about
'her white folks' going to a 'pitcher show' on Sunday!"

"You needn't worry, Mother," said Rita, laughing. "I
wouldn't get her started on religion for anything!' "

As they laughed, the door opened and Mollie came in to pour
hot coffee. Silently she made the rounds, then she set the coffee
pot on the buffet and solemnly announced to the family, "I seed
a pitcher show las' night."

Startled, Ned said, "Why, Mollie, I'm surprised at you! You
always told us it was so sinful!!"

"Hit wuz at de church," defended Mollie, "an' hit won't no
sinful pitcher. Hit wuz all about Jesus an' His Disciples," she
went on, her eyes wide with the excitement of remembering.
"Jesus wuz a-standing' dere preachin' an' His sweet face looked
so purty an' his beautiful white robes wuz flowin' all aroun' Him
—den, all of a sudden, out come Peter!"

At that Ned exploded a mouthful of coffee across the table
as his resounding laughter rang through the house.

Just then the phone rang and Belle said, "Mollie, please answer the phone and find out whom they wish to speak to."

"Yassum," she answered. In a few moments, Mollie returned
and began clearing the table.

"Mollie," said Belle, "who was wanted on the phone?"

Mollie continued removing the breakfast dishes as she replied, "Hit won't fo' you, Miss Belle. Hit wuz fer dat Mr. Anders you rents de front room to."

"Did they leave a message for him?"

"No, Ma'am." Mollie picked up the tray and started toward the kitchen. "I tole her Mr. Anders won't here but I knowed he'd be back 'cause he sleeps wid Miss Belle."

Fortunately, Ned had finished his coffee, as again he roared with laughter. Though Belle was horrified at what Mollie had said—and wondered to whom it had been said—she, too, had to laugh at Mollie's naive and innocent reply.

That night Will did not come home for supper, and Ned and Belle knew that it undoubtedly meant the beginning of another spree. Each day and night of waiting to hear seemed interminable. Ned had been able to learn only that Will and George Rice had been drinking together and had apparently gone on to "greener pastures." A week later a taxi brought Will home, ill and weak. The driver helped get him into the house and to bed. Will was quite sick, and Ned thought it too much for Belle to have to wait on him during the night, so he asked Mollie to stay, which she did.

Will was violently nauseated and thought this time he'd die for sure. He was frightened—so frightened he moaned, "Mollie, pray for me."

Faithful and devoted old Mollie knelt by a chair near Will's bed and started earnestly praying for Mr. Will.

The nausea came again—Will interrupted her—"Hold on there, Mollie, get the slop-jar, quick!"

Mollie ran to the bathroom, brought the slop-jar and held Will's head. Finally he lay back on his pillow—"All right, Mollie, pray some more."

On her knees again, Mollie picked up the prayers where she left off.

"Wait a minute Mollie—I'm sick again."

Back into the bathroom she hurried for the slop-jar!

This over—"Crack down, Mollie, and pray!"—she went on

her knees again. Finally, she'd prayed all she could think of for Mr. Will so she said, "An' oh, Lawd, bless Mr. George Rice, too, an' take de taste o' whisky 'way fum him."

Will interrupted and said, "Hold on there, Mollie; you keep on praying for me and let old George go to hell!"

Midnight came. Mollie said, "Mr. Will, you go to sleep now, 'cause I got to go home."

"No, Mollie," Will pleaded, "you must stay with me all night. For God's sake, don't leave me."

"Mr. Will," Mollie explained, "you know I don' min' waitin' on you, but I cain' stay all night—ever'body in town would be talkin' 'bout me!"

Will's family and friends never let him live that down.

Will's heart was damaged while he had been in the Army in World War I, and after this illness it was in such bad shape he returned to the government hospital for several months. During the years he had been in and out of various government hospitals many times, and each time the family and Sue were filled with renewed hope. But, alas, it was of short duration! After his return from the hospital this time, Sue wrote Ned and asked him if she should return to Will. She received this reply:

DEAR SUE:
Your letters are sad and they touch me deeply. It is not my fault. I did my best. Will realizes he has made a complete fizz from beginning to end. If he has a sane moment it is when he retrospects. Yesterday he asked Rita to help him get you back. Pitiable! Poor boy! Wrecked and lost in the debris of his fallen castles. He is reaching up for the ground to stand on. If he knows what he wants he does not stay of that mind two hours. He is a walking wreck and failure; he is an utter impossibility. He meets himself at every corner and refutes what he swore to yesterday. He is a question mark and its answer. He was through with whisky yesterday—drinking today. So is his life, assertions and denials. Do all things; do nothing. He loves women, all women—any woman—every woman— and yet is it love? Yes, in a way, but damn the way! Whisky has taken him so far down the road he doesn't know the way home, and he is uncertain if he wants to go home—just travel anywhere, somewhere, and it takes him nowhere! Pitiable! Pitiable!

Yet when he is sober and himself he is lovable to everybody. He is a great favorite with young and old, men and women, and a master in the art of winning nurses and widows.

Poor boy! I do believe he wants to do the right thing—I fear he was not a marrying man. Whisky has killed his sensibilities. He floats subject to the ripple of the smallest stream and the modest puff of the zephyr.

If I knew or thought you could find the scattered pieces of this human wreck I would move heaven and earth to get you back. The woman in Georgia has passed, but there are others; one of the name is as good as the same.

"The only Dad you ever had," you say in your letter. Well this old Dad is your Dad yet—he never can his girl forget. God bless you, Sue, I mourn the change which came within our family range. But it affected not my life—to me you'll ever be Will's wife; and I shall always be your Dad—the only one you ever had—or the only one you ever knew—and the sorriest one who ever grew!

I am miserable—hope is gone. Whisky is hell, not war, as Sherman said—war kills, whisky leaves one continuously dying.

In conclusion:

> I reaffirm my love for you
> Same old Dad in the same old way
> And if I knew just what to do
> I would certainly do it—Say?
> If you know, you tell me.

Most lovingly,
DAD

The last few years of Will's life he did check up on drinking and had no more bad sprees.

Sue was with him when he passed away in the Veterans' Hospital in Dublin, Georgia.

# XXVIII

THE NEXT WINTER Mollie had pneumonia. "Miss Belle" had soup and other delicacies prepared for her and saw that she was well cared for by her grandniece. One night Belle walked the few blocks to her house to see how Mollie was. She found her, apparently in a coma. The grandniece and some of her church friends were sitting around the room waiting for the end.

The grandniece said, "Mrs. Blackshear, she don' know nuthin' now."

Belle walked over to the bed and said, "Mollie, this is Miss Belle. I've come to see you."

Mollie's lids fluttered and she whispered, "Purty as a angel and sweet as Hebben."

In a few hours she breathed her last. The Blackshear family was deeply grieved over her death.

After Mollie, Flossie was the Blackshear's servant. In exchange for house rent, she had "washed" for "Miss Annie" for twenty-five years and had continued to do the Blackshear's laundry on the same terms. Now Belle hired her to come to cook breakfast and clean up the house; then she went home to the washing. In the afternoons she returned to prepare dinner. Flossie was a fine cook and a natural-born mimic. She could have made a name for herself on the stage had she had the opportunity.

Flossie had one bad fault—about every two months or so she would go on an alcoholic spree and lay off from work for about a week. Belle was exasperated one day to find that Flossie had taken two quarts of her homemade scuppernong wine that was in the process of being made. She told her: "Leave the house and never put your foot on this lot again!"

Flossie, who had just drunk enough to be impudent, said, "I'se glad to go; don' wanna work fer you nohow."

Six weeks passed. Belle and Rita were worn out having no servant. One morning early, Flossie's voice was heard calling, "Miss Belle!" from the back porch.

"What do you want, Flossie?"

"Breakfus' is ready!"

"All right, Flossie, we'll be ready in a minute!"

Belle was so glad to see her and Flossie was so glad to get back that neither ever mentioned the "firing" and the "impudent" episode.

One Sunday morning at breakfast the family was discussing their new Episcopal minister and how everyone liked him. Flossie said, "We got a fine preacher too—Reverend Brown, and he's so nice! Ef a school teacher comes to our church, he asts the teacher to talk, an' ef 'nother preacher comes he asts him to preach."

The family listened attentively to Flossie who was standing just inside the dining-room door. Her stories never failed to amuse them, and it was obvious that she was more than enthusiastic about Reverend Brown.

Flossie went on with her story, uninterrupted. "Las' Sunday, old John Dan'l, a country preacher, was there. Reverend Brown —he's so nice —he, said, 'Bro' John Dan'l will preach for us today.' Old John he had on a raggedy overcoat an' he looked a sight! But when he got up to preach he took off de old coat, den he looked a little better."

Then, in perfect imitation of the Negro preacher, even to the tones of "Ole Dan'l's" voice, Flossie gave the family his sermon.

"He got up dere, and' he started—'Brudders an' Sisters! Ha! I'se gwine preach to you today about de root! Ha! I ain' gwine to preach about de marriage root—ha! I'se gwine to preach about de root o' David an' de stem o' Jessie—ha!!' Jes' den Sis Theney Johnson, the deaconess in de choir amen corner, stood up an' yelled 'Good Gawdamighty, Brown, make ole Dan'l set down!'

Ever' body in de church started laughin' an' Reverend Brown
say 'Stop dat laughin', dis ain' no pitcher show, an' besides ole
Dan'l's doin' awright!' Reverend Brown he's so nice!"

Flossie laughed with the rest of them as she concluded her
story, and as she turned toward the kitchen she said, almost to
herself, "Reverend Brown, he's so nice!"

CHAPTER

# XXIX

NED AND BELLE seldom left home now, but they still kept "open house," and how they enjoyed the many friends who dropped in to visit. Ned never lost his ability to entertain people, nor Belle her graciousness and queenly manner.

One of Ned's most loyal friends was Mr. Willingham, who visited with him an hour every afternoon from five to six o'clock. Lew Willingham was as staunch a Republican as Ned was a Democrat, and there were many heated, though friendly, political arguments, as well as discussions on all topics of the day. When Landon was candidate against Franklin D. Roosevelt in 1936 the arguments waxed hottest. When the official word came that Roosevelt had carried every state except Maine and Vermont, Ned's laughter was long and loud; but be it said to his credit that when Mr. Willingham came that day for his visit Ned by-passed the subject because his friend's wound was too raw. Not even Mr. Willingham could speak of it.

Mr. Willingham's brother-in-law, Colonel Erwin, was a boyhood friend of Ned's. He lived at Panama City, about an hour's drive from Marianna. Frequently Mr. Willingham would take Ned in his car to visit Colonel Erwin while Mr. Willingham attended to business.

One morning Mr. Willingham came by quite unexpectedly and after greeting Ned rather hurriedly said, "I have business in Panama City today and thought you would like to go to see Colonel Erwin."

Ned was delighted and got up to go to the car, though he

was wearing his "around the house" wash trousers and a white shirt.

Belle said, "Mr. Blackshear, why don't you put on your new suit?"

"Mr. Willingham is in a hurry," he replied, "besides, these clothes are all right, Belle. I never mind wearing old clothes as long as I know I've got a new suit hanging in the closet."

Off he went in his old clothes, though he was, as always, well-groomed and immaculate. Though in his eighties, Ned took a bath, washed his head and shaved himself with a safety razor every morning, feeling for the beard he could not see in the mirror.

Ned's mind remained alert and his keen interest in civic, state and national affairs never lessened. The *Jacksonville Times Union* and radio news broadcasts kept him well-informed. As Lew Willingham drove along the highway to Panama City, Ned brought up the subject of desegregation that was so much in the news at the time. He knew that Lew, a true Southerner in spite of his being a Republican, would be as concerned about this issue as he was.

"What do these Yankee politicians think they can accomplish by outlawing segregation, Lew?" asked Ned.

"It's hard to say, Ned," Willingham replied. "All their pious talk about the 'poor and down-trodden Southern Negroes' makes me sick. They don't even know what they're talking about— why, most of all this propaganda is put out by a bunch of paid employees calling themselves a Society to Uplift and Advance the Negro Race when they have no real interest beyond doing a job and drawing a pay check."

"Well, it's a damn sorry state of affairs," said Ned, "when a handful of men can get a law passed trying to legislate social equality between Negroes and white people. They tried legislating morals with Prohibition and you know what a farce *that* was."

"That I do, Ned, that I do. And if the Supreme Court does outlaw segregation it's going to be even more impossible to enforce, and the bad results more far-reaching."

Ned nodded his head in agreement, as he said, "I pray to God they don't pass it, but if they do—and with all the pressure on them, they might—I just hope that when they realize the infamy of such a decision they'll have the courage to repeal it or reverse their own decision."

"If they pass this thing, Ned, they will have laid the cornerstone for the fall of our nation," Lew said. "Why, man, look at the history books—empires fallen into the dust of oblivion because great nations became rotten to the core with the greed and lust of a few powerful men."

"I know," agreed Ned, "and this desegregation business will be the first blow to the pillars of our government—pillars erected with the blood, sweat and tears of our forefathers. Why, those great men that wrote our Declaration of Independence and the Constitution never dreamed of such a thing!"

They were nearing Panama City now and Lew had to give more attention to the traffic. He turned down the street to Colonel Erwin's and Ned began to look for the house. "Here we are, Lew," he said.

Lew stopped in front of the house and Ned got out of the car. Colonel Erwin, who was sitting on the porch, came down the walk to greet them. Lew said he would be back for Ned about four o'clock that afternoon so they could get home by dark.

Ned thoroughly enjoyed his day with his old friend, talking over old times and eventually politics. The time passed swiftly and almost before he knew it Mr. Willingham was back and it was time to leave.

"Well, Ned, did you have a good day?" Lew asked.

"Splendid, splendid," said Ned, "the Colonel seems to be holding up pretty good for an old man. Hope your business trip was successful."

"Oh, I think it was," Lew said.

"By the way," said Ned, "Colonel Erwin has really been studying up on this desegregation business we were talking about. He's as perturbed about it as the rest of us, of course, and has been writing some articles for the local paper."

"Is that so?" said Lew. "I'd like to read them sometime."

"He showed me some of them. Man, they hit the nail on the head," said Ned enthusiastically. "One of them took the issue straight from the Bible and showed as plain as day that to mix races was not in accordance with God's plan for human beings!"

Lew caught the spark of Ned's enthusiasm." It seems to me I remember something about God's dividing the land among the nations, but I've never been much of a student of the Bible, I'm afraid."

"Neither have I," said Ned, "but the Colonel has really read up on it. I believe what you're thinking about is the story of Noah and his sons—Shem, Japheth and Ham—in the book of Genesis. It seems Ham was disrespectful to Noah and so Noah put a curse on Ham's son, saying, ' A servant of servants shall he be unto his brethren.' I never knew until Colonel told me that the word 'Ham' means dark-colored, swarthy, black."

"I wouldn't have known that either, Ned," said Lew.

"Well, sir, when the flood was over and Noah and all the rest came out of the ark the land was divided among Noah and his three sons, and the Bible said the 'bounds of their habitation' were clearly defined. Ham and his son Canaan were given the land that is now Africa, and that's what Bible scholars believe to be the beginning of the Negro race," Ned went on. "Colonel Erwin had looked all this up and when he was telling me all this I had a faint recollection of my Grandma Pittman reading it to me in the Bible when I was a boy."

"Those things do come back to us," agreed Lew. "I wonder if the members of the Supreme Court wouldn't profit by studying what the Bible says about things like that."

"No doubt about it," Ned agreed, "it sure proves God meant to keep the blacks and whites separated when he sent the blacks to Africa."

"And they'd have been there yet," said Lew, "if Yankee traders hadn't brought them to our southern ports and sold them into slavery to the big plantation owners who needed a lot of help to work all those thousands of acres."

Ned looked thoughtful for a moment, remembering his beloved "Aunt" Martha and "Uncle" Reuben and the other slaves he had known so well in his boyhood on his father's plantation at Frog Level.

"That was sinful—selling and buying human beings, black or white," said Ned, "but the slaves in the old days were well taken care of by their owners and treated with all the respect and dignity that was due them."

"They really were, Ned—though one hears many malicious tales to the contrary," Lew commented, "and they still get good treatment from the people they work for."

"A lot better than they'd ever get up north, by a darned sight," said Ned.

It was almost dusk as they drove up at Ned's house. Both men seemed almost reluctant to reach their destination, so intent had they been on this grave situation.

"Won't you come in, Lew?" Ned asked.

"Better not, Ned—you know, if you aren't on time for meals at a boarding house you're liable to be left out," said Lew.

Ned laughed. "Well, thanks again for the trip. It was a real treat," he said.

"I was glad to have your good company, Ned. Good night, sir. Guess I'll see you tomorrow."

THE NEXT MORNING being Saturday, Ned took his seat on the porch to await Jake's arrival. Jake was a colored Baptist preacher whom Ned had known for a long time. Every Saturday morning Jake came to the back door to "talk things over" with "Mr. Ned." He was often seeking suggestions and ideas for his Sunday sermons, and Ned was glad to help when asked. Jake had a fair education and studied his Bible daily, but in spite of his "schooling" he still had his Negro dialect. As Jake came up on the back porch Ned greeted him with, "Well, Jake, what are you going to preach to your congregation now since the northern politicians are hell-bent on mixing white folks and Negroes like they were all alike?"

Jake scratched his wooly head as he replied, "I'se goin' to tell 'em to be sho' to have God an' de white folks on dere side, but if dey *won't* have God to be sho' dey have de white folks. I'se goin' to tell 'em sech a law would be de worse thing ever happen to us an' dat dem Yankees ought to 'tend to dere own bus'ness 'stead o' tryin' to stir us up an' make trouble where dey ain't none. Dey is meddlin' wid sumpin' dey don' know nuthin' 'bout, nohow!"

With a chuckle, Ned said, "I can't improve on that for your sermon, Jake! It's just right."

Jake went on, "Dem no'the'n folks don' care nuthin' 'bout us nohow, 'cep' to git our vote."

"Why, Jake," Ned admonished him, "they freed your people from slavery, didn't they?"

Jake nodded as he said, "Yassuh, but dey was playin' bofe ends agin the middle. Dey wuz de ones in de fust place who brought us here an' sold us to be slaves; den dey turn on de men what bought us and fit a war to set us free. Dat way, dey couldn' lose fer winnin'.''

Ned chuckled at Jake's vehemence and seriousness, and said, "After they freed the slaves, didn't they take them north and give them good homes and well paying jobs and associate with them?"

"Nawsuh, Mr. Ned," scoffed Jake, "you know dey didn' do nuthin' lak dat! After dey burned dere way through de South an' tuck off mos' ever'thing 'cept de land, dey lef' de slaves for dey white folks to take care of, an' dey done it!"

Ned agreed that this was true, and went on to say, "Since that time the white folks and the Negroes have been working happily together under segregation and have rebuilt a new and richer South. What do your people think started all this up-roar, Jake?"

"I don' rightly know, Mr. Ned," he said, "but I believes a heap of it started when Miz Roosevelt come to Pensacola to talk to de colored Parent-Teachers 'sociation when she read 'em outen de twenty-sixth verse o' Acts that 'God hath made of one blood all nations of men.' Effen she'da read 'em de whole verse stead o' stoppin' at dat comma she woulda tole 'em He also 'determined de bounds of deir habitation.' But she didn't do dat. You know, Mr. Ned, de Devil kin quote Scripture to his own purpose."

"Jake, do your people really want desegregation?" Ned asked. "Do you all want your children to go to our white schools?"

"Mos' of us don't, Mr. Ned, but dere will be some who'll try to force dere way in. An if dey git in dey'll jus' be nobodies 'mongst de white chillun. An' besides dat, our colored teachers will mos' likely lose dey jobs."

"What about going to our churches?"

"Dat ain' no good neither, Mr. Ned," Jake spoke positively. "We all worship God an' hopes to go to Heaven, but our ways o' worship is diffunt. Yawl sits quiet an' listens an' stands still when you sings. We amens and shouts an' claps an' moans, an' we

sways when we sings. Dat's jes' de way God made us. Yo' way
is good fo' you, our way is good fo' us."

"Yes, Jake, and both ways, when sincere, are acceptable to
God."

"Mr. Ned," Jake said earnestly, "dey's a heap o' us colored
folks knows desegregation ain' good for us."

"Do you colored folks believe, Jake," asked Ned, "that the
law can change all the differences and make everybody the
same?"

"Nawsuh, we is too diffunt," Jake replied. "Mos' of us thinks
like you do 'bout this, but dere's always some who don' want
to think right an' won't listen when you try to tell 'em. Some
of 'em acks lak dey's 'shamed to be black, Mr. Ned!"

Ned shook his head in sympathetic understanding. "Being
a Negro is nothing to be ashamed of, Jake," he said, "it is a
noble and ambitious race and possesses many fine qualities. Under
segregation you have produced a lot of fine, outstanding Negro
men and women."

Jake agreed, but added, "I wish dem high-standin' colored
leaders wuz proud enough of the Negro race to fight for segregation for our own sakes."

"They should somehow be made to realize, Jake, that the
majority of the southern Negroes feel that way," said Ned, "and
it would be right for them to fight for equal justice in the courts,
equal wage for equal work and equal but separate chance for education in business and the professions. There are many oppor-
tunities for you to succeed among your own people. Keep your
own schools, teachers, doctors, preachers and churches and have
separate places for recreation."

"Amen, Mr. Ned! I'se goin' to keep talkin' to my people
about it an' I knows we can count on our white folks to help
us."

"That you can, Jake."

"If we don' keep things lak dey is between us, den both
races is goin' to be spoiled," said Jake thoughtfully. "We is lak
two buckets o' paint settin' side by side, one white, the other
black. Effen one drap o' dat black paint gits into de white it

never can be pure white no mo', an' effen a little o' de white is poured into de shiny black paint it turns it a muddy color. Den de white an' de black have done lost dey nachal beauty an' neither one ain' fitten fo' a perfect paint job."

"Jake, that hits the nail right square on the head!"

# XXXI

As Ned turned to leave the back porch he heard a weak distressed call from Belle in the bedroom. Opening the door, he was shocked and frightened to see her on the floor. He hurried to her, thinking she had fallen.

"Don't try to lift me. I was trying to get to the bed, but this weakness came on so fast I eased myself to the floor," she told him.

Flossie and Rita were summoned and the three of them lifted her to the bed. The doctor came quickly and said she had suffered a severe heart attack. Gloom and apprehension settled over the household.

Weak as she was, Belle made valiant efforts to cheer her family. Throughout her two-month illness she retained her delightful sense of humor. She suffered no pain and never complained more than to say, "I'm so tired."

Though she had trained nurses, she liked having Mr. Blackshear and Rita sit in her room most of the time so she could hear and join in their conversations.

A coal fire was kept in the grate in her room day and night. Naturally, ashes accumulated fast and had to be taken out often. One night after supper Ned called Flossie and said, "Get the scuttle and take out these ashes before you go home."

"Nawsuh," she replied, "I ain' gwine take up no ashes."

"What do you mean, Flossie," he said in a stern voice, "don't you know I won't stand for such impudence? You take up those ashes!"

"Yassuh."

She shoveled the ashes into the scuttle, put the iron front back in place, brushed up the hearth, picked up the scuttle and started out. At the door she turned and, rolling her eyes like she was frightened, said, "Mr. Blackshear, you made me take up dem ashes an' you knowed it's bad luck to take up ashes after sundown."

"Bad luck!" Ned said in a loud voice. "Bad luck! Why in the devil didn't you say it was bad luck! Put those ashes back in the fireplace!"

She did and they were both happy.

Belle, weak as she was, almost shook the bed with her laughter as she said, "Mr. Blackshear, we never could get those Negro superstitions out of you!"

But superstitions, prayers, doctors and loving care were to no avail. She finally was just too tired. After a reign of more than half a century as queen of Ned's heart and home she relinquished her scepter and slipped quietly away to rest. Ned laid her beside their boys in the Episcopal churchyard in Marianna.

After leaving the churchyard, a sad Ned and Rita sat together in the living room. Rita, reaching to pat his hand, said, "Daddy, I shall take care of you."

"Thank God I have you, Daughter, but how can I get along without Belle?"

The evening shadows were now fast lengthening for Ned, but he had behind him nearly a century of joyous living. Rita was his constant and loving companion for the next eight months. Never was she tired or bored with listening to the tales of his early youth and later incidents in his life with which he entertained her.

As they sat after supper one night Ned said, "Daughter, there is one sin I'm afraid God will not forgive me for."

Startled, Rita said, "Good gracious, Daddy, what terrible thing did you do?"

"I know I was called to preach and I didn't do it."

Greatly relieved, she replied, "Why, Daddy, you have always preached; your whole life has been a sermon, with life's stage as your pulpit. You have enriched every life fortunate

enough to touch yours, and you have scattered sunshine wherever you've been. Maybe that is the way God meant for you
to answer your call to preach, but if not, I believe He will compromise with you on that score."

He smiled with the old twinkle in his eye and said, "I hope
you are right. God knows I'm sorry for my sins."

"Come now, Daddy, it's time for a 'man of your rank and
smell' to be tucked into bed."

Just before the Supreme Court handed down its decision on
segregation (infamous decision, he would have called it), Rita
"tucked him in to bed" for the last time. He was not ill; he
simply could not go on without Belle.

As he "crossed the bar," he heard familiar Negro voices
singing "Swing low, sweet chariot, comin' for to carry me
home," and he saw his little Belle coming to meet him. It was
a glorious reunion.

Then, hand in hand, they walked toward the Negro quarter
to find old Uncle Reuben. Marse Ned wanted to console the old
darkie for what the Yankees were still trying to do to his noble
race and to his beloved Southern white folks.

TO E. J. BLACKSHEAR

He has followed the trail into the sunset,
And on to the sunrise above.
He's wending his way, a song in his heart,
To a kingdom whose watchword is love,
Over the golden heights,
Down to the crystal sea,
Holding fast to his loving heart
Memories of you and me.